The WORLD'S BEST STREET & YARD GAMES

• • • • •

Written & Illustrated by
Glen Vecchione

 Sterling Publishing Co., Inc.   New York

In the Same Series
The World's Best Party Games
The World's Best Travel Games

Library of Congress Cataloging-in-Publication Data

Vecchione, Glen.
  The world's best street & yard games / by Glen
Vecchione.
    p.   cm.
  Includes index.
  Summary: Presents instructions for approximately
100 outdoor action games filled with chases, surprises,
and good-natured roughhousing for all ages.
  ISBN 0-8069-6900-8
  1. Games—Juvenile literature. [1. Games.] I. Title.
II. Title: World's best street and yard games.
GV1203.V38 1989
796'.01'922—dc19   88-38273
                  CIP
                  AC

Copyright © 1989 by Glen Vecchione
Published by Sterling Publishing Co., Inc.
Two Park Avenue, New York, N.Y. 10016
Distributed in Canada by Oak Tree Press Ltd.
% Canadian Manda Group, P.O. Box 920, Station U
Toronto, Ontario, Canada M8Z 5P9
Distributed in Great Britain and Europe by Cassell PLC
Artillery House, Artillery Row, London SW1P 1RT, England
Distributed in Australia by Capricorn Ltd.
P.O. Box 665, Lane Cove, NSW 2066
Manufactured in the United States of America

90-1257

Contents

To my mother and father

Before You Begin

Outdoor games are action games. And for a day of fun and fast-paced excitement, nothing can compare with them. The games in this book are our personal favorites—filled with chases and surprises and good-natured roughhousing for all ages.

You'll find well-known games like "Ringelevio," and some unusual—though equally entertaining—games such as "Aliens" and "Treasure Maze," played very far away and long ago.

There are classics like "Run, Sheepy, Run" that threaten to pass into obscurity, which would be a shame, because they're so much fun.

And there are many other games so imaginative and appealing, with such special and unusual charms, that any lover of outdoor games—regardless of age—will be instantly drawn in.

All the games are challenging and amusing, without being hurtful physically or emotionally. You can play most of them with mixed groups of girls and boys from age 8 up, and adults are enthusiastic players of almost every one. We've included a few games for younger children, too. If in doubt about any game, check the age range chart in the back of the book.

Specific requirements for each game are listed right at the start, so that you can see at a glance how many people you need and what kind of space is required. A few of the games are designed for just one or two players, but most of them call for groups and some can expand to accommodate large numbers. Unless otherwise noted, the standard playing area for each game is roughly the size of a volleyball court (60′ × 30′). If any game needs a larger or more complex field, that information is listed under "Special."

One word of caution: the words "street games" may conjure up affectionate recollections for some people, but today's streets aren't like the streets of 40 years ago. In those days, even some of the liveliest neighborhoods had little more than the Good Humor truck to rattle the calm of a summer evening. Unfortunately, times have changed, and it isn't safe these days to play games on any ordinary street. There are plenty of options, though.

In many parts of the country developers and urban planners have introduced "play streets"—closed streets and intersections having all the authenticity of the real thing, except for cars. These streets are excellent for the majority of the games in this book. However, many of the games don't call for streets at all—they can be played on any paved surface. You can play many of them on both paved *and* grassy surfaces—near lamp posts or lawn ornaments, in schoolyards or backyards—the choice is yours.

And so, here are the games—collected, adapted, re-invented and even a few created from scratch—from someone who played them all—and remembers.

1
Tag & Tag Again

Most outdoor games are tag games in one way or another. In its simplest form, tag is a contest between fast and nimble runners. In more developed versions, it can be a tightly organized game of teams, bases, and strategies. But the idea is always the same: a player—or group of players—is chosen to be "It." "It" chases the other players and tags them, either "capturing" a running player or making that player the new "It". The game continues until everyone is either captured or tired out. That's all there is to it—but what a variety of games you find!

Freeze Tag

Players: 7–15
Materials: None
Surface: Paved or grassy

Freeze tag is one of the easiest and funniest tag games. It's good to play with lots of people, because the more players involved, the more unpredictable and surprising the game becomes. When you're "It," you chase the other players, trying to tag each one. When a player is tagged, he freezes and must wait for an un-tagged player to tag and un-freeze him. You win if you manage to freeze everyone. You lose if some of your friends are still running around and you're just too tired to play anymore!

There is one exception to the freeze rule. It's called "Electricity," and it comes into play when several frozen players are within touching distance of each other. One of the players calls "Electricity," and then all the frozen players link hands. Then if one player should be un-tagged, everyone in the chain is free as well. It can seem as if all is lost in one of these games until "Electricity" is called and one brave player saves the day!

Shadow Tag

Players: 4–10
Materials: None
Surface: Paved or grassy

The twist in this tag game is that "It" has to step on the shadow of a runner to tag him. Of course, playing at different times of day will have different results—high noon and small shadows make for a harder game, and late afternoon gives "It" a decided advantage.

The interesting thing about "Shadow Tag" is that you get involved in a whole new way of running. If "It" stands in front of you, but your shadow lies behind, you can practically march up to "It" and tweek his nose! Watching out for your shadow instead of yourself also makes for collisions between players—so be careful.

Shadow Freeze Tag

In this variation, "It" tags your back to freeze you, but any other player can tag your shadow to un-freeze you. At first, it might seem easier tagging shadows than backs, but that all depends on the time of day!

Statue Tag

Players: 5–10
Materials: None
Surface: Paved or grassy

"Statue Tag" will remind you a little of "Freeze Tag," but it's slightly crazier—and as much fun to watch as it is to play! "It" chases the other players, as usual. When a player is tagged, he freezes, but cannot be un-frozen by a running player. Eventually, all the running players are frozen and the second part of the game begins. "It" goes to each frozen player, takes him by the arm, spins him around and then lets him go. Whatever position a player falls in he keeps—each freezing into a strange statue. "It" then chooses the most unusual statue to take his place in the next game.

Touch Tag

Players: 5–10
Materials: None
Surface: Paved or grassy
Special: An area that has some variety to it—trees,
             bushes, a lamp post or hydrant—they'll all
             come in handy.

In this game, "It" chases the other players, but calls out
something they may touch to be safe from tagging. "It"
may call out "Wood!", in which case every running
player needs to grab hold of something wooden—a tree
trunk or fence, for example—for safety. Or maybe the
next time "It" might call out "Metal!", and the players
would scramble to the closest parked car or lamp post.
A player may not share a space with another player. Any
player running from place to place is free to be tagged,
especially the poor player who can't find safety because
all the safe spots have been taken by friends!
　　Tagged players are out of the game. The last player
to be tagged is "It" in the next round.

Pantomime Tag

Players: 4–10
Materials: Chalk or rope
Surface: Paved or grassy
Special: A slightly larger playing area with a few
             obstacles (such as lamp posts or trees) to
             make the chase more challenging.

Choose two teams and mark out a den. One team—the

"Ins"—remains in the den while the other team, the "Outs," stands outside facing it.

The Outs choose an activity to pantomime, something that is definite, but allows for some variety. For example, if the team agrees to "saw wood," each player might saw wood differently, some with the left arm and some with the right. Or suppose the activity is "watching T.V." Some players might sit up to watch while others lie on the floor; some might switch channels while others just stare.

When the Ins guess the activity, they run out of the den and try to tag the Outs. If caught, they become Ins for the next round.

Soon there are more Ins than Outs. After the last player is tagged, divide up sides and start again.

Trivia Quiz Tag

Players: 7–10
Materials: None
Surface: Paved or grassy

This one will have you hitting the books after school is out. The player who is "It" chooses a subject, preferably one that the other players are familiar with. It could be something like "Indian Tribes," or "Makes of Cars," or "Cartoon Characters." Then "It" begins chasing the others, but when a player is about to be tagged, he may call out any name in his category—"Iroquois!" or "Duesenberg!" or "Fred Flintstone!"—to remain safe. An answer may be used only once, and "It" may change the subject as often as he pleases. Of course, any player who is tagged becomes "It" for the next round and gets to choose his own subject.

You might want to try using such trivia subjects as "John Wayne Movies" or "What Mr. Spock said to Captain Kirk"—if you're playing with some really sharp company!

Chinese Tag

Players:	**5–10**
Materials:	**None**
Surface:	**Paved or grassy**

Nobody knows how this tag game got its name, but don't let that stop you from giving it a try.

Whenever "It" tags a player, that player not only becomes "It," but must also place his hand over the part of his body that was tagged. So if Nancy was tagged on the shoulder, she places a hand on her shoulder and has to tag someone else without using that hand. If she manages to tag John on the knee, she is no longer "It" and can remove her hand from her shoulder. Now, John—hand on knee—hobbles after her and anyone else nearby. "It" may use only his free hand to tag another player, but depending on where the other hand is placed, he may find it difficult to get around. Try chasing someone with your hand stuck to your toe!

Squat Tag

Players: 5–10
Materials: None
Surface: Paved or grassy

Most of the rules for this game are right in the name. Each player has to squat when "It" approaches to keep from being tagged. This can force "It" to be a little sneakier than usual. Creeping up behind a player—or chasing a player, only to turn suddenly and spring for another—is highly recommended!

2
Chases, Races, Hiding Places

There's no doubt about it—chasing and being chased is fun! So is hiding, and—well, maybe not *quite* so much fun—looking for someone. The chasing and hiding games in this chapter have some unusual and unexpected twists. A few games combine elements of both chasing *and* hiding. Some are old and some are new—all are fun!

Four Corner Upset

Players: 5
Materials: Chalk
Surface: Paved
Special: "Street" intersection with four sidewalk
corners (optional)

If you can find two intersecting streets, both of which
have been closed off to traffic, set your game up there.
The game loses none of its spunk, however, if you play it
on a chalked surface. Simply draw the four corners,
making sure they're at least 25 feet apart. Then draw a
small base on each corner.

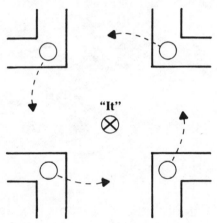

Four of the five players stand on the corner bases
while the fifth player—"It"—stands in the center of the
intersection. "It" calls out, "I want a corner. Give me
yours!" and then points to one of the other players. If
that player chooses to, he may surrender his corner and
change places with "It." More often, though, none of the
players wants to give up a corner and "It" is forced to
say: "I'm *upset!*" At that, each player switches corners

with the player to his right. "It" tries to rush in and claim a corner for himself.

It's fun if "It" tries to fool the others into running. He can do this by calling out, "I'm up—*sidedown!*" or "I'm up—*a tree!*" If a player has the jitters, or just isn't listening carefully enough, he may run away from his corner and find he has nowhere to go!

Play until all players have had a chance to be "It."

Detective's Trail

Players: 2
Materials: 2 paper bags
Strips of paper or brightly colored stones
Surface: Paved or grassy
Special: A large and not necessarily flat area with lots of nooks and crannies

Mark off one small area as home base or "Robber's Den" and choose one player to be "It." "It" goes off while the other player covers his eyes and counts to 100. The unusual part of this game is that "It" takes along a bag filled with strips of paper or colored stones or any other kind of marker, and leaves a trail for the other player to follow. The trail may wind around the block, or in and out of doorways, or up and down stairs, and it should be as complicated as possible!

The object of the game is for "It" to get back to the den before the other player catches up. "It" doesn't hide, but tries to keep far ahead of the detective. This is easier said than done because "It" must always leave a trail, even when he's making a dash for it. And the detective must always stick to the trail and pick up every marker, even when he can see "It" close up ahead.

Streets and Alleys

Players: 18–30, but always an even number
Materials: None
Surface: Paved or grassy

"Streets and Alleys" is a great tag game for large groups. It is always unpredictable and makes for lots of laughs as the chaser and the chased stumble around their friends in a mad dash for home base.

First select a small area on the ground to be home base. It can be any spot you decide upon, but should be clearly marked. Then choose one player to be chased, and another to do the chasing. The remaining players stand side by side in several equal lines, one line beside the other. There should be at least four players in each line, with at least four lines in all. Each player in line links hands with the players standing alongside him, forming "streets." A player in one of the lines becomes the Caller, and when he shouts "Alleys!", all players drop hands, make a quarter turn to the right, and link hands with the new players standing on either side. This turns the "streets" into "alleys." It's a good idea to practice this with your Caller for a while, so there won't be too much confusion when the game gets going.

Let's say you're the chased player. You get a short head start and your destination is home base, at the other end of all the "streets." As you start down through the first street, weaving your way home, the chaser sets after you. But it's not so easy! Just as the chase starts heating up, the caller yells "Alleys!" and everyone in line turns, making for a whole new situation! You have to figure out a new strategy, a new direction, and avoid the chaser at the same time.

If you get to home base without being tagged, you may either start running again or choose another player from the line to take your place. The chaser must keep going, though, until he tags somebody.

Gee

Players:	**10–20**
Materials:	**Chalk or 2 ropes for marking out a den and a prison**
Surface:	**Paved or grassy**
Special:	**A large area needed, with plenty of hiding places**

Divide the players into two teams and draw a den and a prison, each large enough to hold an entire team. Team

#1 goes off to hide. Team #2 waits behind in the den, counting to 100 with eyes closed.

At the count of 100, Team #2 sets out to find Team #1. When a seeker spots a hider, he shouts "Gee!" The hider jumps out and chases all the seekers back to the den, trying to tag as many possible. Tagged seekers must go to prison, but if all the seekers make it back to the den without being tagged, the hider goes to prison.

The next time you play, reverse the sides. Play the same way as before, but when seekers are tagged, they can be *exchanged* for prisoners taken in the previous round. So if Team #2 has had three players in prison from the last round, and Team #1 has two players tagged in this round, two of Team #2's prisoners may be exchanged for Team #1 prisoners, and only the third prisoner remains.

The game continues until one team gets the other team completely "behind bars."

Fish in the Basket

Players: 8–12
Materials: Chalk
Surface: Paved

This court game from Asia combines strategy with some fast running. Choose four players to be Fishermen. They position themselves on the playing court like this:

Fishermen #1, #2, and #3 take the horizontal lines, while Fisherman #4 takes the vertical line in the center. Fishermen may only run back and forth on their lines, while the other players—the Fish—may use the whole playing area (A).

The object of the game is for the Fish to run from one end of the court to the other, and back again. The Fishermen run along the lines as they try to trap all the Fish in one square. They would do this by surrounding them on three sides (B).

When a Fish makes it across and back again, he may call out "Ice!", which makes everyone freeze. This allows each remaining Fish to take one giant step in any direction, while the Fishermen may only watch. Then a Fisherman calls, "Fire!" and the chase resumes.

The "Ice/Fire" rule is a handy one, particularly when only one Fish is left on the court and is about to be surrounded. If another Fish shouts, "Ice" in time, the threatened Fish is sometimes able to take one step out of the square and into a safer place. Yelling "Ice" is allowed only once per Fish, however. A Fish usually saves it until he spots real trouble.

The game continues until the last Fish is caught, or until all make it back safely.

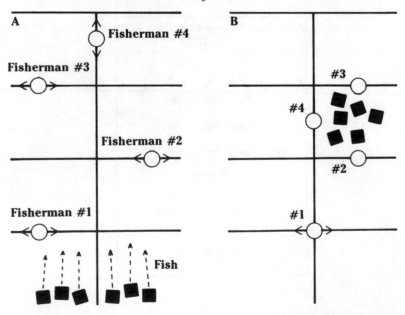

Carpenters and Coalmen _____

Players: 11–21
Materials: Chalk or rope
Surface: Paved or grassy
Special: A large area, free of obstacles

Carpinteros (car-pin-TA-ros) means "carpenters" in Spanish, and *carboneros* (car-bo-NA-ros) means "coalmen." For this game to work, you have to learn those words, as well as another: *cardenales* (car-di-NA-les), which means "cardinals."

Draw two boundary lines, about 100 feet apart. Choose a leader and divide the remaining players into two teams—*Carpinteros* and *Carboneros*—that face each other in parallel lines. Each team stands about 40 feet from its boundary line, facing away from it.

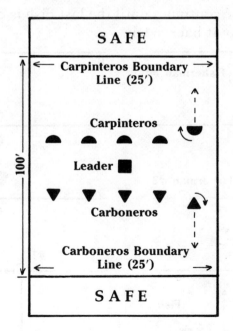

The leader stands between the teams and calls out the name of one of them. If he calls *"Carboneros!"* the coalmen turn and run for their boundary line, the *Carpinteros* in hot pursuit. If the *Carpinteros* manage to tag a player, he or she is taken out of the game. If the leader calls out *"Carpinteros!"* the situation is reversed.

The leader may also call out *"Cardenales!"* or rather: "CARRR-*denales*," which is used to make everyone very nervous because neither team may stir. A mere twitch gets you eliminated!

A team wins when it annihilates the competition.

Dove and Hawk _____

Players: 6–12
Materials: None
Surface: Paved or grassy

Don't let the appealing title of this Chinese tag game fool you—"Dove and Hawk" can get pretty intense, even among the best of friends. A group of three steps out from the other players. The player in the middle is the Dove Owner, a person of Royal ancestry. To her right is the Dove, to her left the Hawk. She makes a motion as if throwing the Dove in the air, and the player to her right runs off. After a moment or two, she whistles, releasing the Hawk. The player to her left now runs off to tag— and devour—the Dove.

The Dove Owner watches the chase quietly. When she tires of the entertainment, she claps her hands and the Dove returns to the safety of her right side. If she thinks the Dove has performed well, she spares him and places him in a "Golden Cage." If not, he is sent out again after a short rest. The Dove Owner sometimes lets the chase go on too long, in which case the tired Dove is "devoured" by the Hawk and neither returns. When this happens, the Dove Owner chooses a new Dove and Hawk from among the remaining players.

It all sounds very tame. That is, except for the fact that players often alternate screams of, "Why didn't you fly faster?" with shouts of, "Why didn't you call me in sooner?" The game continues until many of the Doves have been devoured by the Hawks. Then Dove Owner walks to the Golden Cage and quietly admires her favorites. . . .

Sardines

Players: 5–10
Materials: Chalk or rope
Surface: Paved or grassy
Special: A moderately large area with lots of "nooks" and "crannies"

This is hide-and-seek backwards, with a good chase at the end. Mark out home base—or choose any clearly marked spot for it. Select one player to be "It," but in this game "It" hides while *the others* count to 50. When the count is through, the players go out in search of "It," quickly separating from each other to look thoroughly in every part of the area. When one of the searchers spots "It," however, he doesn't tag her or call out to the others, but instead joins her in her space, squeezing in like a sardine next to her. As the remaining searchers discover the hiders, each squeezes into the hiding place. Everyone must now be especially quiet so as not to alert the remaining searchers (easier said than done!)

The hiding players wait for the last searching player, who is usually getting pretty nervous by this time. When he finally discovers the hiding sardines, they all jump out and race for home base. The last player to reach home base is "It" in the next game.

Search Party

Players: 10–20, but always an even number
Materials: Chalk or rope
Surface: Paved or grassy
Special: A large area needed, with plenty of variety and good places to hide

Mark out a home base or "camp." Form two teams that will take turns being the hikers and the searchers.

Before the action begins, the first team to hike secretly selects one member who will be "lost" on the trip and not return with the others. Then the hikers set out while the searchers wait at home base.

When the hikers return, the searchers first try to figure out who has disappeared, and then set out to find him.

Meanwhile, the "lost" hiker tries to evade the searchers and get safely back to camp. If he gets back to his team, all the hikers call out "Safety!" and the searchers return to the camp. Then the safe member of the hiking team picks a member of the searching team to be taken out of the game—usually the best player!

If, on the other hand, the lost player is discovered by the searching team, he is taken out of the game. The game starts again, with the searchers becoming the hikers.

Hikers and searchers take turns hiding people until one unfortunate team vanishes altogether!

Smugglers

Players:	**10–20, but always an even number**
Materials:	**A key, stone, coin, or any other small object**
	Chalk or rope for marking out a Den
Surface:	**Paved or grassy**
Special:	**A large—not necessarily flat—area to make the chase more interesting**

You need two teams for this game: the "Ins" and the "Outs". The Ins have a Den while the Outs plan their strategy in the field.

One member of the Outs has the "jewel," which can be a key, a stone, a coin—anything small enough to be hidden in the palm of your hand. The identity of the player who carries the jewel must remain a closely guarded secret among teammates.

The Ins count to 50 while the Outs move farther and farther away. After the count is finished, the Ins yell, "Smugglers!", and the chase is on. As each member of the

Out team is tagged, he must open his hands to show whether or not he has the jewel. Of course, the jewel should be passed around among teammates as quickly and as inconspicuously as possible. There are lots of opportunities for playing the decoy in this game!

When the holder of the jewel is tagged, the game is over and the sides change.

Smuggler Elimination Game

You may want to try playing with the rule that a tagged player without the jewel is taken out of the game. This makes for fewer and fewer players on the out team, and it becomes more difficult to smuggle the jewel undetected. But if tagged players are allowed to stay in the game and keep running, you'll get some interesting results, because the jewel can continue to be passed almost anywhere. Your choice!

I Spy

Players:	6–20
Material:	Chalk or rope
Surface:	Paved or grassy
Special:	A large area needed, with plenty of hiding places

This basic hide-and-seek game is a favorite of anyone who loves to play outdoors.

Mark out a home base with chalk or with rope. The base should be large enough to contain all the players. One player—"It"—steps out of home base and counts:

"One potato, two potato,
Three potato, four—
Five potato, six potato,
Seven potato, more!"

While "It" is counting, the other players run off to hide. "It" should be sure to give the players enough time to find good hiding places. When finished counting, "It" calls out, "Ready or not, here I come!" and then goes off to search for the hiders.

When "It" sees a hiding player—Jack, for instance—he tries to act as if nothing has happened as he calmly walks back to home base. Once there, he cries out, "I spy Jack behind the lamp post!" Jack then surrenders and is placed in home base as a prisoner. But if Jack knows—by "It"'s reaction—that he has been discovered, he may choose to jump out of hiding and race to the safety of home base before "It" gets there.

The game continues as "It" spies hiders, taking prisoners—or as hiders race "It" to home base. Any player who loses the race is taken prisoner and placed in home base while "It" continues to look for the other players. "It" must also keep an eye on home base, however, because another hider may rush out to tag (and release) the prisoners. If this happens, both the prisoner and his rescuer sneak off to hide again.

One other rule: If "It" claims to spy someone and is wrong—about who or where—the hider named does not need to surrender.

The game continues until "It" spies all the hiders and takes them prisoner, or until all the hiders are safe. Usually, the last player spied becomes the next "It".

3
One Against Many

You may not think it's much fun when your friends gang up on you, but these games just might change your mind. A few of them "turn the tables" on the usual idea that the many have the advantage over the few. In some, you're the absolute and uncontested authority as to who may approach and who must stay behind. But in others, it's you against the crowd!

Blindman's Buff

Players: 4–10
Materials: A blindfold
Surface: Paved or grassy

This is probably one of the oldest games of all time, and it really hasn't changed much over the years. Just imagine this: you'll be playing the ten-zillionth game of "Blindman's Buff" in almost exactly the same way people played it more than a thousand years ago!

Blindfold one of the players and spin him around three times. The blindfolded player tries to tag one of the other players, who may tease and taunt him. For instance, the other players may crouch low, sneak up behind the "Blindman" and yell "Boo!", or stand still and keep very quiet.

Eventually though, someone will get careless and be tagged. That player is then blindfolded for the next game.

Hen and Chicks

Players: 6–12
Materials: None
Surface: Paved or grassy

One player is the Hen, another the Fox. They should be fairly evenly matched. The remaining players are the chicks. They line up behind the Hen, holding waists or shoulders.

Fox marches up to Hen and says: "Mother Hen, your chicks look good today." Hen replies: "Mr. Fox, go away!"

Fox then tries to capture the last chick by pulling her from the line, while Hen tries to protect her. The other chicks can join in by wrapping themselves around the threatened chick, but the line must never break apart. If it does, Fox may tag any (and all) of them.

Each time a chick is captured, it is out of the game—placed in Fox's "cooking pot." The game ends when all the chicks are captured.

Buzzzz

Players: **10–20, but always an even number**
Materials: **Chalk or rope**
Surface: **Paved or grassy**

Divide the players into two teams and draw a long line separating them. Team #1 sends a player into Team #2 territory, and he tags as many Team #2 players as he can. While he is tagging them, he must make the sound *"Buzzzz"* in one long continuous breath—loud enough for everyone to hear. If the tagger can make it back across the line to his own team without running out of breath, the players he tagged are out of the game. But if Team #2 holds him long enough—by grabbing his arms or legs or pinning him to the ground—he runs out of breath and is eliminated, himself.

Teams take turns sending a player into enemy territory. The first team to annihilate the other wins.

Dancing Bear

Players: 5–10
Materials: A rope (about 10 to 15 feet long is best), and something to tie it to
Surface: Paved or grassy
Special: An area with something—a tree, fence, or lamp post—to tie the rope to

Tie one end of the rope to a tree, fence or lamp post—anything strong enough to withstand some sharp tugs. The player chosen to be the "Dancing Bear" must hold the other end of the rope with one hand as he tries to tag the other players with his free hand. The other players taunt the Bear by moving within touching distance. When a player is tagged, he becomes a Bear too, joining hands with the original Bear, and helping to tag the rest of the players.

The Bear can be pretty tricky in this game: it may perform a little dance that amuses everyone and then suddenly jump out to tag a player. Or it may run around a player or stand close by and ensnare him. Never underestimate a dancing bear!

Uncle Sam

Players: 4–10
Materials: Chalk or rope
Surface: Paved or grassy

Choose one player to be Uncle Sam, who stands behind a boundary line. The other players stand facing Uncle Sam from behind a second boundary line about 20 yards away. Player #1 calls out:

"Uncle Sam, Uncle Sam
May I come across your dam?"

Uncle Sam replies with:

"Not unless you have the color ——"

and he chooses a color, usually one that the player is wearing very little of—just to make life difficult.

If Player #1 is wearing the color named by Uncle Sam, he's allowed to take one giant step closer to Sam's line. If not, he stays put. Players take turns asking Sam if they may cross, and each time Sam may ask for a different color. This is a game of favorites: Sam may choose to let a player get closer and closer, and then stall him for a long while.

When a player gets *too* close, Sam may start asking for some exotic colors to forestall being tagged. But a player can outsmart him—filling a pocket with colored buttons, for example.

The first player to cross Sam's boundary line and tag him becomes the new Uncle Sam. A player may also try to *dash* across—if he thinks Sam is not paying attention. But should Sam see him coming and call "Out!" before he reaches the other side, that player is eliminated from the game.

Red Light, Green Light

Players: 5–10
Materials: Chalk or rope
Surface: Paved or grassy

One player—"It"—moves about 15 feet away from the others, who stand in a row behind a starting line.

"It" turns his back to the others and calls "Green Light," at which point the players run towards him. After a few seconds, he calls, "Red Light," which tells the running players they must stop and freeze in position. "It" then whirls around to face the players, and tries to catch someone moving. If caught, that player must go back to the starting line.

Each time "It" turns his back and calls "Green Light," the players run closer. As they close in, "It" usually makes green lights shorter and red lights longer, hoping to catch the closest player and send him back to the starting line.

The player that manages to tag "It" becomes "It" in the next game.

4
Old Favorites

These are the games that practically everyone knows and loves—the ones with those familiar chants and arguments, usually begun in that all-too-short hour before suppertime, and resumed happily later on. Some, like "Prisoner's Base," "Ringelevio," and "Run, Sheepy, Run," are tag games that call for teams and a little more space for playing. Others, like "Angel and Devil," are quieter and may be played in smaller areas. All of them eat up lots of energy—so get ready!

Red Rover

Players: 7–20
Materials: Chalk or 2 ropes (for marking out boundary lines)
Surface: Paved or grassy
Special: Large area needed

Red Rover is one of the classic street games. Some versions are nearly 700 years old!

Divide a 100-foot-long stretch of the street into three equal areas. The outer areas are Dens, while the middle area is occupied by a single player. The other players may go into either Den—it's up to each individual player to choose which Den to start out from.

All the players wait in their Dens until the middle player begins the game by calling: "Red Rover, come on over!" Then all run from their Dens across the middle area to seek safety in the opposite Den. The middle player tries to capture one of the players by holding him and counting to ten. If he succeeds, the captured player remains in the middle and helps capture the remaining players in the next round.

The middle players call, "Red Rover, come on over!" a second time, and the remaining players run across again. As you can see, each time the call is repeated, more players are captured, and fewer players are left to occupy the Dens. This may result in one Den being left empty. If this happens, one of the middle players may rush into the empty Den and shout, "Take base 1-2-3!" three times. From that point on, the game is slightly different. Middle players, still in position, are now allowed to choose individual players to run across their territory. If one very fast runner is particularly irksome to the middle players, you can bet they'll pick him first to run across. That player may ask for "protection"—that is, he may ask up to three other runners to surround him as he makes a dash for it, but no player has to help him.

When the last runner is captured by the middle players, the game is over. Usually this last runner, by virtue of his skill and longevity, gets to choose someone to call, "Red Rover, come on over" and begin the next game.

Kick the Can

Players:	4–10
Materials:	Chalk
	Empty tin can
Surface:	Paved
Special:	Large and varied playing area needed for this one—with plenty of hiding places

This beloved game of city kids has been around for a very long time. Draw a circle about six feet in diameter and place an empty tin can in the center. Choose one player to be "It," who stands inside the circle guarding the can as the others players wait outside. Suddenly, one of the outside players rushes into the circle and kicks the can as far as possible. The others then run and hide, except for "It," who must fetch the can and carry it back to the circle before yelling "Freeze!"

Players must stop where they are after "It" yells "Freeze!" "It" can call the name of any player he sees, forcing that player to stand beside the circle as prisoner. "It" then carefully ventures out to find the hidden players, but this is dangerous. A player may rush out of hiding at any time and kick the can again, freeing all prisoners—who will no doubt rush off to hide. Of course, "It" must fetch the can again, which gives the running players time to hide—and the hiding players a chance to switch places, all the while creeping closer to the circle.

If *and only if* there are no prisoners, a player may make a dash for the circle. If he gets inside before "It" can tag him, he shouts, "Home free!" and everyone, including "It," runs to the circle. Of course, if the player is tagged, he's taken prisoner.

The last one inside the circle after "Home free" is "It" for the next game.

Ringelevio 1-2-3

Players: 10–30, but always an even number
Materials: Chalk or rope
Surface: Paved or grassy
Special: Large area, with a few small obstacles, such as trees, bushes, hydrants, etc.

You need lots of room for this rough-and-tumble tag game. The teams need to do some fast running.

Select two teams and mark out a Den that is large enough to hold an entire team. One team goes out while the other—the "It" team—stays near, but not inside the Den. The "It" team chooses one of its members to guard the Den, which is done by keeping one foot inside the Den at all times.

The game begins when the "It" team starts counting to 100, giving the field team enough time to run far away from the Den. When the count is finished, the "It" team shouts, "Ready or not, here we come!" and everyone on the team, except for the Den Guard, runs after the others.

To capture a player, a member of the "It" team must grab and hold onto his victim long enough to call out, "Ringelevio 1-2-3!" three times. If the victim breaks away before the repetition is completed, he may continue running. If he's captured, however, he's placed in the Den and made a prisoner.

Captured players remain in the Den until tagged by a teammate. They may also break out if the Den Guard accidentally takes one foot out of the Den or places *both* feet inside it. Prisoners may try to pull the Guard inside, or push him out, or they may just wait to be rescued.

If an "It" player gets tired, he can stand alongside the Den next to the Guard. But if that tired player steps into the Den accidentally, or is pulled into it by one of the prisoners, the prisoner may shout out "Two Guards!", and win his own release.

When all the members of the field team are captured, the game is over. Change sides for the next game.

Prisoner's Base

Players: 10–30, but always an even number
Materials: Chalk or 3 ropes (for marking out home bases and a prison)
Surface: Paved or grassy
Special: A large area needed, with a few small obstacles—such as trees, bushes, or lamp posts—to make the chase more interesting

This tag game is so old it is even described in one of Shakespeare's plays. It was once outlawed, because it became so popular that it interfered with the king's walks to and from Parliament! You won't have to worry about that, but after trying it, you'll see why it's still such a favorite.

There are two teams, each with its own home base. Also mark out a prison—both teams will use it.

The members of each team link hands, stretching out from their home bases. The last in the chain (the one farthest from the base) breaks away and runs into the field. Then the last link on the opposite team's chain breaks away and chases him. While that chase goes on, the players continue to break from their team's chain and pair off with a member of the opposite team. In this way, each chaser has a particular player he must tag.

When a player is tagged, he goes to prison and his captor stands guard. The prisoner can be released only if a member of his own team runs through the prison and tags him. Of course, the guard watches for this and may tag any would-be rescuer. If several players of the same team are in prison, they may call out "Electricity!" and join hands, stretching a chain out and away from the prison boundaries. A teammate may touch the last person in the chain and release all the prisoners.

The game is finished when all the members of the first team are captured.

Run, Sheepy, Run _____

Players: 10–20, but always an even number
Materials: Chalk or rope
Surface: Paved or grassy
Special: A large playing area, with many good places to hide

Try this game if you like signals and secret codes. Divide the players into two teams and mark out two home bases. Also mark out a prison, which should be far away from each home base. In this game, one team hides and then tries to go back to home base before the other team can find and capture its members. Both teams choose captains who direct the hiding and searching.

Before you start, the captain of the hiders decides on a secret code that will allow him to communicate important information to his teammates. Some codewords might be:

Bloodhound, which means: **They're closing in on you, keep low and stay quiet.**

or

Grandma, which means: **"It's safe to start crawling towards home now."**

or

House on Fire, which means: **"Run for it!"**

He can make up as many codewords as he'd like, but it's best to keep them simple to avoid confusion.

After the hiding team learns the code, the captain announces that his team is ready to hide. The "It" team waits at home base and doesn't look. Meanwhile, the captain of the hiders goes with the members of his team and notes their hiding places. Team members should hide fairly close together so that they can hear the codewords. When everyone is hidden, the captain of the hiders returns the "It" team and announces that all is ready.

The search begins. Both team captains take part: the captain of the "It" team leads the search, and the captain of the hiders calls out codewords to teammates, trying to maneuver them closer to home. He tells them when it's safe to creep forward or better to stay back. The captain of the "It" team may try to confuse the hiding players by calling out the same codewords!

If one of the hiders is discovered by a member of the "It" team, the hider is "captured" and placed in prison.

Captured players are released only when tagged by a teammate.

When the captain of the hiders feels he has guided his team close enough to home, he calls out, "Run, Sheepy, Run!", which means that everyone can come out of hiding and make a run for it. It also means that the search is over, and the "It" team must also run for home. Captured players in prison must be tagged and released by their teammates at this point. The first team to get all of its players safely within home base wins the game.

The captain of the "It" team may call out, "Run, Sheepy, Run!" too. He may do this if he feels his team is in a better position to win the race for home, which might be the case if some of the fastest runners on the hiding team have been captured.

Teams take turns being the hiders and the searchers. And of course, for each game a new secret code has to be invented.

Jump Rope

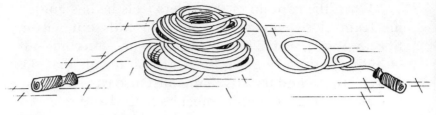

Players: 1–10
Materials: **Short jump rope (about 5 feet long)**
            Clothesline (at least 20 feet long)
Surface: **Paved**

Jumping rope is terrific exercise and a great test of skill and coordination. In old-fashioned May Day celebrations at village fairs, as many as ten people could be seen jumping over one long rope, but you don't often see anything that elaborate these days.

You can jump alone or with a partner, using a short store-bought jumping rope. Or, you can jump inside a longer clothesline, turned by two friends. There are two classes of games. The first consists of fancy jumping, chasing and dancing routines. Here are just a few:

Rock the Cradle: Rock the rope back and forth instead of revolving it. You can do this alone on a short rope, or you can do it on a longer rope letting the turners "rock" for you. It's a great way to warm up!

Wind the Clock: While the rope is turning count from 1 to 12, making a quarter turn clockwise each time. Again, you can do it alone or with two friends turning for you.

Visiting: One player starts jumping alone, turning her own rope. Another player jumps in and faces her, "visiting" for a while, before jumping out again.

Chasing: This involves two turners and at least two jumpers. The first jumper enters, jumps over the rope once, and then rushes out as the second jumper enters, and so on.

Square Dancing: Two players turn while two jumpers link arms and do a "Do-se-do"—all the while jumping!

Hopping: Two players turn as the jumper rushes in and hops, alternating legs for each turn of the rope. After 10 hops, the jumper runs out and is replaced by another jumper.

The second class of games consists of rhymes—recited by either the turners or the jumpers. There are many of these, and some are much more complicated than others—but most of them fall into one of the following groups:

Counting Rhymes

These are rhymes that end with counting to test how long a jumper can keep going. You can chant them alone, or have the turners chant for you. One popular counting rhyme goes like this:

Fire, fire, house on fire—
Mrs. Sweeny climbed up higher,
There she met the Fireman Steve—
How many kisses did she receive?
One, two, three, four, five, six. . . .

Alphabet Rhymes

The jumper or turners chant the alphabet at the end of
these rhymes—the letter the jumper stumbles on means
something very important—it's usually the first initial
of your sweetheart, whether you know it or not!

Strawberry shortcake, cream on top
Tell me the name of my sweetheart
A, B, C, D, E. . . .

Switching Rhymes

These are short rhymes that call for the old jumper to
move out and a new one to come in. They are usually
chanted by the turners.

My mother and your mother
Live across the way,
Every night they have a fight
And this is what they say:
Acka baka soda cracker
Acka baka boo
Acka baka soda cracker
Out goes you!

In addition to the two basic kinds of jump rope games,

there are many ways to *turn* the rope. This can make an already difficult game even more challenging. If you have a very long clothesline, for example, you can turn it into two jump ropes. The clothesline is doubled over—one turner holds the two ends, while the other turner wraps the rope around her back, over her forearms, and through her hands. Now you're ready for "Double Dutch" and "French Dutch."

"Double Dutch" is a technique where the two ropes are turned *toward* each other—but carefully—so that they don't collide. The result is a kind of "egg-beater," that leaves the poor jumper quite exhausted after a short time!

In "French Dutch," the ropes are turned *away* from each other—again, very carefully—with similar results. If this isn't difficult enough, you can try both "Double Dutch" and "French Dutch" with a dose of "Hot Pepper." This merely means turning the ropes as fast as possible—until someone cries, "Help!"

Chinese Jump Rope

Players: 4–8

Materials: "Rope" made from rubberbands (Chinese jump ropes are inexpensive and available at most novelty stores)

Surface: Paved

"Chinese Jump Rope" isn't really a jumping rope game at all. It may remind you more of "Cat's Cradle," the hand game of fancy string designs. The "rope" is actually a loop made from hundreds of rubberbands, braided together.

Players #1 and #2 stand facing each other with their feet apart and the rope around their ankles. They back away from each other far enough for the rope to stretch tightly and lift off the sidewalk.

Player #3 jumps between them, placing her feet apart. At the same time, Player #1 jumps out—now the rope is stretched between Players #3 and #2. Soon Player #4 jumps in, taking the place of Player #2. All the while, the rope must remain tightly stretched and off the ground.

At this point, things get a little more complicated. Players #1 and #2 jump back into the rope, as Players #3 and #4 jump out. Then Players #3 and #4 switch places with #1 and #2 again. Timing is very important!

Jumping in and out at exactly the right moment keeps the rope stretched. One miscalculation makes for a snapped rope or a tripped player!

Making Shapes—A Variation

If you have a very long rope, you can make shapes to jump in and out of. Three players can stretch the rope into a triangle. One by one, each player is replaced by a player from outside. Then a *fourth* player jumps in and turns the triangle into a square. One by one, those players are replaced until a *fifth* player turns the square into a pentagon.

The sequence is then reversed and the players create simpler shapes. This creates a special problem: three of the five pentagon players are each replaced, but the last two jump out *together*—replaced by a single player. In this way, the pentagon turns back into a square, and the square becomes a triangle again.

There are no winners or losers in "Chinese Jump Rope," and no points to be gained. But it's a challenging game of skill and coordination, and it's great fun to watch!

Four Coin Toss _____

Players: 3–7
Materials: Chalk
             4 coins for each player
Surface: Paved

This game was popular when Charles Dickens was a boy, and many parents complained that their children idled away too many hours playing it!

Draw a circle about six inches in diameter. Then draw a starting line about five feet away from it. The players must stand behind this line. Each player has four coins, and takes a turn pitching one coin towards the circle. The player coming closest to the center of the circle takes all the other thrown coins and is allowed to take one step closer to the circle. In this new position, he tosses all his coins towards the circle at once, keeping the ones that clearly fall inside. The coins that fall outside the circle are gathered up by the next player, who also takes a step forward before tossing all of *his* coins. Any coins from outside the circle are then gathered up by the third player, who takes a step forward, and so on.

Each time a player takes a turn, he steps closer to the circle. Soon, players surround the circle and no more steps can be taken. But the coin tossing continues until one player bankrupts all the others.

Angel and Devil

Players: 8–20
Materials: Chalk
          Rope (for Tug-of-War)
Surface: Paved or grassy

This game is a favorite in Mexico. During the fiesta season, you'll often see costumed players engaged in a colorful game of *Angel y Diablo*.

Choose someone to be the "Angel" and someone to be the "Devil." The remaining players are "Souls," and agree among themselves on a secret color-name for each. Then they stand in a line facing the Angel and Devil.

The Angel waves its arms like wings, then stops and pretends to knock at a door.

The Souls say: "Who is there?"

The Angel replies: "A lonely angel seeking company."

The Souls ask: "Who will you take with you?"

The Angel replies, "I will take Blue!"

The Soul named Blue leaves the others and "flies" away with the Angel.

Now it's the Devil's turn. He asks the same questions, and demands another color. The player named joins the Devil. If the Devil chooses a color that no one has taken, he may not claim a player in this turn. This holds true for the Angel as well.

This continues until all the Souls have joined either the Angel or the Devil. Then, a line is drawn on the ground and there is a tug-of-war. The first side to drag the other side over the line, wins.

What's the Time?

Players: 7–15
Materials: Chalk or rope
Surface: Paved or grassy
Special: Larger area needed

This guessing game has a fun chase at the end. Two of the players secretly agree upon a time of day. They also secretly agree on which of them is "A.M." and which is "P.M." The remaining players stand in a row. Mark out home base about 100 feet away.

One of the two players walks along the row asking each person: "What's the time?" The second player stands beside the questioner and watches.

Players take turns guessing any hour or half hour within a 24-hour period, specifying "A.M." or "P.M." Let's say the correct answer is 8 A.M. and the player guesses it. Then, the P.M. player shouts "Go!" and the guesser leaps out of line to chase A.M. to home base. If the correct answer is 8 P.M., the A.M. player shouts "Go!" and the guesser chases after the P.M. player.

If either A.M. or P.M. is tagged before reaching home base, the tagger takes his place. If neither is caught, A.M. and P.M. secretly agree on a new time and a new round begins. Continue playing until everyone has had a chance to be A.M. or P.M.

5
All in a Circle

Circle games have been around a long time. Once
the polite form of play for little children—and
well-dressed ladies and gentlemen at garden par-
ties—the games have come a long way. Now circle games include races and tags and wrap-
around horseplay. And in this chapter you'll find
another sort of game—"All Sewn Up"—which is
a kind of mathematical chase-and-capture. The
Victorians were unacquainted with such games,
and would *not have been amused!*

Cat and Mouse

Players: 10–20
Materials: None
Surface: Paved or grassy

This game is also called "Thread the Needle," and after trying it, you'll see why. One player is the Mouse. The other players form a circle, linking hands and holding them up high enough for Cat and Mouse to pass under.

Mouse walks around the outside of the circle. Then suddenly it tags one of the others and rushes away. The player tagged becomes the Cat and must chase Mouse as it weaves in and out of the circle, under the arms of the other players. Cat must follow Mouse's moves exactly and cannot take shortcuts across the circle.

If Mouse is caught, it joins the others in the circle and Cat becomes the new Mouse.

Duck, Duck, Goose

Players: 10–20
Materials: None
Surface: Paved or grassy

This game keeps you alert! The players sit in a circle facing in. "It" walks around the outside of the circle, stopping here and there to tap a sitting player and say, "Duck." This often goes on for a while as "It" waits for his friends to relax so he can catch them off guard.

Suddenly "It" taps a player, yells "Goose!" and rushes away. The tagged player must leap up and race around the circle in the opposite direction to reclaim his space. That is, unless, "It" gets there first!

The player left without a space in the circle becomes "It" in the next round.

The Wolf and the Sheep

Players: 10–20
Materials: None
Surface: Paved or grassy

Choose one player to be the "Wolf," and another to be the "Sheep." The remaining players join hands and form a circle around the Sheep, protecting her.

The Wolf creeps around the outside of the circle and tries to break through while the others do their best to keep him out. The Wolf might try crawling under the legs of the defending players, or he may run as fast as he can and throw himself against the line. Defensive maneuvers might include bunching up around the Sheep to keep her snug, or fanning out and running around to keep the strongest players circulating. Any strategy the players come up with is legal so long as their hands remain linked.

When the Wolf breaks through the circle, he grabs the Sheep's hand and tries to break out with her. Again, the players in the circle try to prevent this. They may close in tightly around the Wolf to separate him from his catch, or lift their arms to let the Wolf out, and then whip them down before he can pull the Sheep through!

If the Wolf manages to pull the Sheep through the circle, then they both join the circle and choose two new players to be Wolf and Sheep.

Twos and Threes _____

Players: 20–30
Materials: None
Surface: Paved or grassy

This game seems complicated at first, but learning it is well worth the trouble. It's especially good for the quick of mind and fleet of foot, and guaranteed to work up a good appetite for supper!

Players form two circles, one inside the other. Each circle should have the same number of people, so that pairs of players are formed between the inside and outside circles. There should be enough room between the pairs of players for people to pass through on either side.

Begin the game by having one player—called the

"Pea"—stand at the center of the circles, while another player, called the "Bogey," stands outside. Pea walks slowly around inside the inner circle, finally stopping in front of someone, so that now there are three players standing in a row: Pea; the player on the inside circle; and the player on the outside circle.

Now the outside player must run, pursued by the Bogey, who had been waiting for this to happen. The outside player is only safe if he can become a Pea—that is, get into the center of the circles and stand beside an inside player, turning a line of "twos" into "threes" again so that a different outside player is displaced.

Both Bogey and the chased player may run in and out between the pairs of players in the circles, but the Bogey will want to remain outside much of the time—to be in a better position to tag a player bumped from the outside circle.

When the Bogey tags a player, he rejoins the circle. The tagged player becomes the Bogey and gets to choose a new Pea to start the game again.

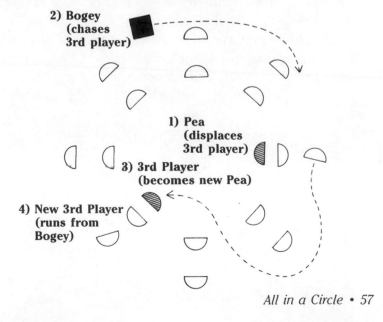

2) Bogey (chases 3rd player)

1) Pea (displaces 3rd player)

3) 3rd Player (becomes new Pea)

4) New 3rd Player (runs from Bogey)

All Sewn Up

Players: 10–20
Materials: None
Surface: Paved or grassy

This unusual chase game has a mathematical twist. Players stand in a circle, leaving enough space between each player for another player to pass through. Two players, let's say Eric and Joan, stand in the center.

On the word "Go!", Eric and Joan separate and run between the standing players, weaving in and out of the circle. Each time either one passes between two standing players, the players link hands and close up the space, so the circle is gradually "sewn up."

Eric's goal is to sew up the circle and capture Joan inside. He must calculate his moves carefully though, or he may sew himself up too! Or, he may find to his dismay, that she's outside and he's inside! Joan has the same plan. Both players must watch carefully and try to keep just one step ahead of each other—that's what makes this game so challenging.

Should both players be sewn up together, they must repeat the game until one is captured. The captured player joins the circle and chooses a replacement.

6
Roughhouse Games

Sometimes, you just have to cut loose. Some of the games in this chapter, like "Johnny on a Pony," may be familiar. Others, like "The Snake Eats Its Tail," may be a new experience—but all are about really rough playing—nothing hurtful or dangerous, but certainly rough-and-tumble. For this reason, the directions—particularly regarding the surface a game is played on—should be followed exactly.

Johnny on a Pony

Players: At least 10, but always an even number
Materials: None
Surface: Grassy (with a strong tree or wall nearby)

Divide players evenly into two sides. On one side, players bend over in a line holding waists, with the first player in line bracing himself against a wall or tree trunk. This is the "Pony."

One by one, players on the other side jump onto the back of the Pony and wriggle forward to tag the first player in line. Players in the Pony try to shake each rider off before he reaches the first in line, but the Pony must never break apart or collapse.

If the rider makes it far enough to tag the first in line, he gets one point. If thrown off, that player goes to the back of his own team's line and the Pony gets a point. When three points are scored by either side, that team wins and the sides are reversed.

Bull in the Pen

Players: 10–20
Materials: None
Surface: Grassy

One player is the "Bull." The remaining players join hands and surround him in a circle. The object of the game is for the Bull to break out of his pen and reach the safety of home base before he's tagged by another player. You can locate home base about 50 feet away if you have many players and the circle is very large; but only about 20 to 30 feet away if a smaller group is playing.

You might think that all there is to this game is a lot of pushing and shoving, but the Bull can use brainwork, too. As the Bull, for example, you should be clever enough to know that a quick duck under two players' arms (or a surprise dive over them, for that matter!) can win your release. The Bull can be cute, too. How about getting a wary player to scratch your ear while you have your eye on the fellow who's yawning on the other side? There are many possibilities.

If the Bull gets out of his pen and makes it to home base without being tagged, he can either choose to be the Bull again or have another player take his place. If the Bull is tagged, the one who tagged him gets to be the Bull in the next game.

King of the Ring ⸻

Players: 4–7
Materials: Chalk
Surface: Paved

Draw a circle about five feet in diameter and stand in the center. As the "King," you have to protect yourself against invaders who enter the circle and try to drag you out. Only one invader at a time may enter, and anything goes: pushing, shoving, tripping, lifting up and carrying—whatever! You'll soon be exhausted enough to *want* out (that is, after you've tried to hold on to your kingdom for a while). If two invaders enter, you may call, "Foul!" and take one out of the game. And if three try to gang up on you, you may call "Double foul!" and remove two of them.

Continue playing until everyone has a chance to be King.

Chicken Fight ⸻

Players: 4–10, but always an even number
Materials: None
Surface: Grassy

For this game, players pair up, and the smaller player climbs onto the shoulders of the larger one. Together, they are the "Chicken." Several Chickens prepare for battle by strutting around, looking ferocious.

Suddenly, one Chicken charges another. The players underneath do the running and backing away, while the top players push and pull each other. The object is to knock a top player off the shoulders of his partner.

If you're playing with more than two Chickens, you may want to fight two at a time, and then re-match the winners—or you can enjoy a free-for-all Chicken fight!

The Snake Eats His Tail _____

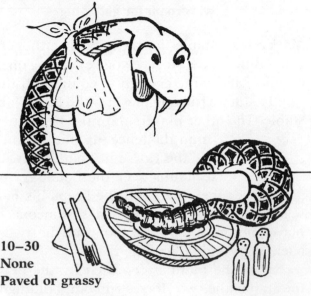

Players: 10–30
Materials: None
Surface: Paved or grassy

The "Snake" has some unexpected twists and turns. Everyone joins hands, making a long line. Or, if you prefer, you can hold waists or shoulders instead—it doesn't really matter. The idea of this game is that the head of this Snake (the first person in line) tries to tag the last player in line, eliminating him. The players in between squirm around, trying to keep head and tail apart. Any player who breaks the line is out.

The game continues until the Snake swallows the last morsel of tail, or until everyone is too dizzy to go on playing.

Ride the Horse

Players: 6–15
Materials: Chalk or rope
Surface: Paved or grassy
Special: You might want a little more space for this one. Make sure the area is clear and level with room for galloping.

Mark out a "Stable" for the horse in either chalk or rope, depending on the surface you're playing on. It should be circular, and large enough to contain all the players.

To start with, one player—the Horse—occupies the stable. The other players dare the Horse to break out:

"Jump the fence, up and down,
Ride the Horse to London town!"

The Horse jumps over the boundary of his stable and chases the others, but he keeps his hands clasped together in front until he tags someone. The tagged player becomes a Horse too, and the two Horses run back to the stable together.

After the taunt is repeated by the players outside the stable, the two Horses run out, holding hands, until one of them tags a third player. Then all *three* Horses run back—but separately now—to the stable. This time, any of the un-tagged players may jump on their backs and ride them!

If a Horse carries a rider all the way into the stable, the player is captured and becomes a Horse. For each round, the Horses run out, holding hands. But whenever they tag a player, the chain breaks apart and the Horses race back individually, ridden by un-tagged players. Play until all the riders turn into Horses.

7

Chalk on the Sidewalk

The games people get the most nostalgic about
are probably those scrawled onto the pavement
with colored chalk. Every neighborhood seems
to have its share of strange charts and arrows,
mysterious symbols and squiggles, peculiar pat-
terns and tracks! In this chapter, you'll find some
of the more familiar games, and a few less com-
mon variations. Remember—they need only a
paved surface, and, like all the other games,
should *never* be played in a street that hasn't
been closed off to traffic.

Hopscotch

Players: 2–6
Materials: Chalk
Small stone or coin
for each player
Surface: Paved

A

7	8
6	
4	5
3	
1	2

The game of hopscotch is very old and has many variations. You can even see the remains of hopscotch boards scratched into the ancient streets of the Roman Forum! You might know hopscotch by another name, "Potsy." This name probably came about because small pieces of pottery were once tossed onto the board instead of the bottletop or skate key that was used in the 1930's and 40's.

Hopscotch is an interesting game because it tests your skill and coordination. Some board designs are simple and others are more complex, but they all work the same way: You throw a small object into the first square, hop over that square and through the board to the highest numbered square. Then you turn and hop back through the board. You finish by picking up the object from the first square and hopping *over* it and out.

Let's take an example. If you're playing on an ordinary board (A), you start out by standing at the foot of the board and tossing your "Pot" into the #1 square. If it lands clearly inside, you hop on your right foot into the #2 square, and then into the #3 square. At this point you jump so that you land with your left foot in #4 and your right foot in #5. Then you hop on your right foot into #6, and jump again, landing with your left foot in #7 and your right foot in #8. Now it's time to return. You jump and twist around so that you land facing your "Pot"—your *left* foot in #8 and your *right* foot in #7. You hop on your *left* foot into #6; jump and land with your left foot in #5 and your right foot in #4; hop on your left foot into #3; and then into #2. Before you hop out though, you must lean over and pick up your "Pot" from square #1.

Players take turns throwing the "Pot" into higher and higher numbered spaces. If a player steps on a line, or trips, or if a throw misses its space, the turn passes to the next player. The first player to hop through the full sequence of numbers wins the game.

Some boards are designed with neighboring squares so that you may take turns hopping and jumping (landing on both feet, each one in a separate square).

Territory Hopscotch

Another more elaborate version of Hopscotch uses the "Territory" rule. After you hop through the board successfully and are standing outside it, you turn your back to it, and toss your coin or stone over your shoulder. Where it lands becomes your "territory," and you write your initials in the corner of the square. The other players may not throw or hop in this square now, which complicates things for everyone! You win if you accumulate more territories than your opponents, or eliminate them by owning enough squares to make hopping too difficult. If you miss the mark, or stumble as you try to hop across squares, you are out of the game.

Round Hopscotch

Hopscotch was made for variation. Here are two more designs:

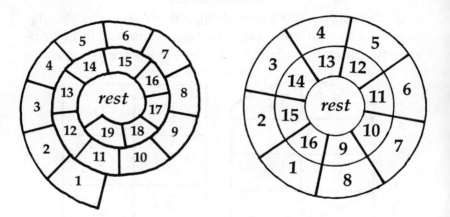

Try designing your own hopscotch board. It's still hopscotch as long as you keep to the basic rules of the game.

Skully

Players: 2–7
Materials: Chalk
Bottlecaps or checkers
Chewing gum (optional)
Surface: Paved (and smooth)

"Skully" is a little like "Marbles," except that you play with bottlecaps or checkers. If you're smart, you'll have some sticky chewing gum around for this one (it'll come in handy later). Draw a board no more than five feet from end to end. Make sure the pavement you draw on isn't too bumpy to skate a bottlecap across!

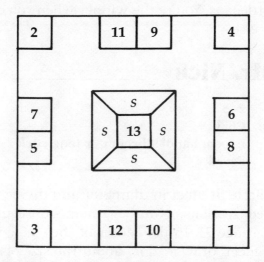

The object here is to flick (snap your index finger out from under your thumb) a bottlecap from Box #1 all the way to Box #13, and then back to Box #1 again. When you return to Box #1, you become a "Killer" and can take a player out of the game by bumping his bottlecap with yours.

You begin the game by taking turns flicking a bottlecap through the board from square to square. You are not allowed to take shortcuts through the other squares. Surrounding Box #13 are four "Skull Zones." If you land in any one of them, you must go through the other three before you can enter Box #13.

If you can possibly bump another player's bottlecap, it is highly recommended. That not only knocks him out of position, but it gives you an extra turn. However, you may "gum your cap" (or checker) to keep it sticking to the pavement when you see trouble coming, and then remove the gum when it's your turn to shoot. It's perfectly legal!

Often, the last stages of the game involve several Killer bottlecaps. You're the winner when you eliminate everyone else.

Old Mr. Nick _____

Players: 2–5
Materials: Chalk
                 Broom handle, broom or long stick
Surface: Paved

Draw a circle five feet in diameter and divide it into 16 pie-shaped sections. Number them consecutively, as shown on page 71. In the center of the circle where all the lines meet, draw a "dot" about the size of a quarter and fill it in with chalk.

Player #1 stands at the edge of the circle holding the broomstick. The other players blindfold him, and stand the broomstick in Section #1. Then everyone backs away as Player #1, moving only his broomstick, taps around the circle reciting:

Old Mr. Nick
Tapped on his stick
Twenty times 'round
Before he found
The center ground!

Player #1 taps the stick once for each syllable. On the word "ground," he tries to place his stick on the center dot for a 20-point bonus. If the blindfolded player misses the center but hits one of the numbered slices instead, he receives the number of points in that slice, and the section is crossed out or "taken."

Player #2 goes through the same routine. If she too misses the center point, she crosses out the slice her stick landed in and claims those points. However, if her stick lands in the section that was "taken" by Player #1, she gets no points and loses her turn. This also happens if the stick winds up on a line between sections or outside the circle altogether.

When all the sections have been crossed out, the players add up their scores. The one with the most points wins.

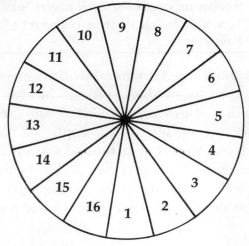

Nine Men's Morris

Players: 2
Materials: Chalk
   9 coins or stones for each player (players must be able to tell their pieces apart)
Surface: Paved

How old is this game? It was a favorite among country folk during the time of Shakespeare, who even mentions it by name in *A Midsummer Night's Dream*. Supposedly, Shakespeare himself was an accomplished player!

"Nine Men's Morris" may remind you a little of "Tic-Tac-Toe" or checkers, but it has a charm all its own. Draw a board consisting of three concentric squares. Each square should contain eight dots (for a total of 24 dots).

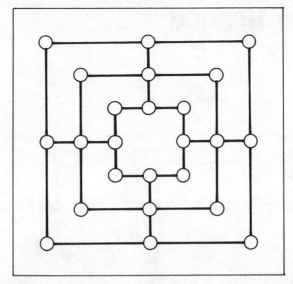

The players each have nine coins or stones that they take turns placing one by one, over the dots. Make sure that whatever pieces you use for playing are easy to distinguish from your opponent's pieces.

When you finish placing all the pieces on the board, take turns moving your pieces to neighboring empty points. The object is to form a row of three—either diagonally or along the side of a square—without being blocked by an opponent.

When you form a row of three, you may remove one of your opponent's pieces from the board. This holds true only for unconnected pieces. Once a player forms a row of three, no pieces of it may be removed. There is one exception to this rule: a piece may be removed from a row *if no other pieces are available*. When this happens, the game is over and the player who has lost the piece loses the game. Another way to win is to block all of your opponent's men, making it impossible for him to move.

Crazy Highway

Players: 5–10
Materials: Chalk
Surface: Paved

"X" marks the spot where the "Line Painter" begins. She walks backwards, turns this way and that, and drags a piece of chalk along the pavement. Player #1 counts to 10 and then follows this "crazy highway" wherever it goes. Player #2 counts to 10 and then follows #1. Player #3 counts to 10 and then follows #2— and so on.

As the line of players gets longer, it speeds up, gaining on the Painter. But she suddenly turns and intersects the line, making a second "X." Player #1 stops there, gets off the line, and begins again from the first "X." Player #2 passes the spot and begins gaining on the

Painter. But she intersects the line a second time. Now Player #2 must stop and go back to the first "X" too.

And it continues. At each new intersection the next player in line must stop and go back to the beginning. In this way, the Painter keeps slightly ahead of the players chasing her. But a player only has to stop at an intersection once. After each player gets back in line, it's a smooth ride and a fast chase. If the Painter is tagged, she's *out*, and the player who tagged her becomes the Painter in the next game. If she manages to reconnect her line to the first "X"—finishing the large "circle"—everyone has to reverse direction, and she races back along the highway to tag the others.

Each player now races back to the intersection where he first stopped. From here, he jumps off the highway to "safety in the center." If a player is tagged before he can reach safety, he becomes the Painter in the next game. If all players jump off the highway before any one of them is tagged, the Painter repeats her role in the next game.

Fox and Geese

Players: **5–10**
Materials: **Chalk**
Surface: **Paved**

This is a great game to play at the beach or in the snow, but a street or schoolyard will do just fine.

One player is the Fox and the rest are geese. Draw a large circle on the ground (about 30 feet in diameter) and divide it up so that it looks like a huge wagon wheel with six spokes. The center of the wheel where the spokes meet is home base.

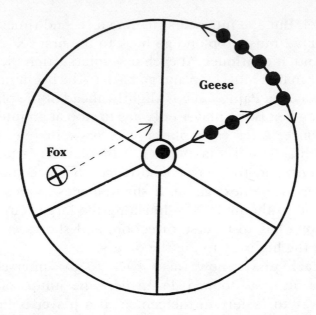

The object of the game is for the Fox to chase the geese and tag them as they run around the hub of the wheel and along the spokes. The geese may run in any direction, and may even jump across the spokes if they have to, but they must follow the lines of the wheel. A tired goose may seek safety in home base for a little while, but when a second goose enters, the first must leave. The Fox chases the geese by running inside the circle in whatever direction he pleases, but he must not touch the lines.

Any goose tagged by the Fox is out of the game. When the last goose is caught, the game is over. Choose a new Fox.

8
Ball Games

Outdoor ball games are plentiful and varied. Besides some of the more familiar ones like "Stoop Ball," "Dodge Ball," and "Seven Up," you'll find a few unusual ones here too, like "Chinese Handball" and "Four Square." Some games require 2 or more players, while others may be played alone. Some use pavement alone as a playing surface while a few require a high wall. The game "I Declare War" is in a class of its own—but it's an all-time favorite and, like the others, loads of fun.

Dodge-Ball _____

Players: 6–20, but always an even number
Materials: Chalk
Large soft ball
Surface: Paved
Special: Large, clear playing area

"Dodge-Ball" will be familiar to anyone who has had to spend a rainy hour in the gym, but it's a great game for outdoors, too. All you need is a wide area and a large ball. A basketball will do in a pinch, but one of those softer plastic "kick-balls" is better (and safer) for throwing point-blank at your opponent.

Draw two parallel lines about 30 feet long each, one for each team. Extending the length of the line, and about 15 feet behind it, is the "Target Zone." Separating the two Target Zones is a neutral area about 100 feet long where only the player holding the ball may go.

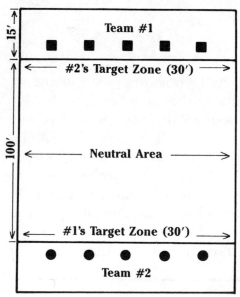

Players take turns heaving the ball to the opposite side in an attempt to hit a player on the other team, taking him out of the game. Be careful to aim for the legs and feet of the player, not head and chest. If a player catches the ball, then the *thrower* is taken out of the game. Continue until one team has been annihilated.

Apartments

Players: 6
Materials: **Chalk**
                  Small rubber ball
Surface: **Paved**
Special: **High wall**

You can play this scaled-down version of "Dodge-Ball" with six people, a wall, and a smaller ball. Five players stand against the wall, about five feet apart, separated by chalk lines drawn up the wall. The sixth player, who stands about thirty feet away, throws the ball at any one of them. A player may twist and duck out of the way, but he may not leave his "apartment." If he's hit, it's one count against him. Three counts and he's out of the game. If a player catches the ball, he changes places with the thrower, who has to take on all the counts against him as well. The last remaining player wins.

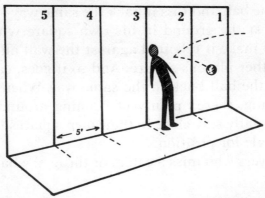

Chinese Handball

Players: 5
Materials: Ball
Chalk
Surface: Paved
Special: Wall behind playing area

Divide the space directly in front of the wall into five sections, each one about four feet square. Or, if the pavement is divided into squares, let each player take a square.

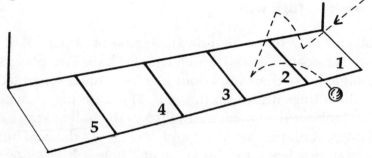

Players stand back about five feet from their squares. The player in Square #1 begins the game by slamming the ball against the ground in his own square so that it bounces up, ricochets against the wall, and bounces in another player's square. That player must catch the ball and toss it back the same way—throwing it against the ground in his own square with enough force to make it rebound against the wall and fall into some other player's square. And so it goes, each player hitting the ball back in the same way. When the game gets going, there's plenty of running around—players don't usually stay close to their own squares for long as they angle for position.

Players who miss a catch, or throw the ball without

bouncing it first, are eliminated from the game and the remaining players move one square to the right. The last remaining player is the winner.

Kings

This variation—"Kings"—is played for points. Player #1 stands behind the first square and throws the ball into Player #2's square, hitting the sidewalk first and then the wall. Player #3 throws the ball to Player #4 the same way, who throws it to Player #5, who returns it to Player #4, and so on. Any player who fumbles a throw or a catch receives one count against him. Eleven counts takes him out of the game, and the remaining players move one square to the right. The player who eliminates all the others and winds up in the first square is called the "King."

Home Runs _____

Players:	**6 (3 to a team)**
Materials:	**Ball**
Surface:	**Paved**
Special:	**Stoop**

"Home Runs" is a short version of baseball, played against a stoop. One player stands in the street just beyond the curb, facing the stoop. He is the batter. Two teammates stand about 15 feet behind him, as do all three players from the other team.

The batter throws the ball against the stoop with as much or as little force as he wishes. A bounce on the sidewalk counts as a strike; one bounce in the street, a single; two bounces, a double; three bounces, a triple;

and four bounces, a home run. If the ball is caught by someone on the other team, it counts as an automatic *out* and the teams switch sides.

Keep in mind that no ball may be caught on the fly in "Home Runs." A ball must bounce at least once before it counts for anything. If your team is at bat, it can be tough deciding whether to let the ball keep bouncing and risk having the other team nab it, or snap it up quickly and settle for a lowly single.

Monday, Tuesday

Players:	7
Materials:	Ball
Surface:	Paved
Special:	High wall

Here's a game to test your reflexes. Play it when you're razor-sharp and full of energy!

Each player takes the name of a day in the week. The first player ("Friday") throws the ball against the ground as hard as possible so that it bounces up and rebounds against the wall. At the same time, Friday shouts out the day-name of another player—"Wednesday," let's say—who must catch the ball after the first bounce and send it back in the same way, calling out the name of another player.

If Wednesday misses the catch, everyone scatters except Wednesday, who must now retrieve the ball and tag one of the others. The tagged player is next to throw the ball against the ground, but the tag counts as a mark against him. Three tags and a player is out of the game altogether. The game continues until only one player is left—the winner.

Stoop-Ball

Players: 1 or 2
Materials: Ball
              Chalk
Surface: Paved
Special: Stoop

"Stoop-Ball" is a great game for a lazy afternoon. You can play it alone or with a partner. If you're playing by yourself, stand in the street a few feet from the curb and throw the ball at the stoop. There are two ways to score:

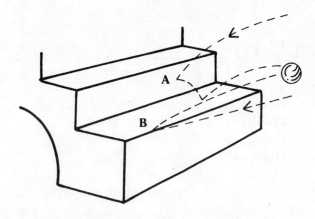

(A) **Riser ball**: The ball hits the back of the step (the *riser*), ricochets back down against the step, and you catch it on the fly. This earns you one point.

(B) **Corner ball**: The ball hits the corner where the step and the riser join, bounces back, and you catch it on the fly. This earns you 10 points.

Each time your throw goes any other way, or if you fail to catch the ball on the fly, the stoop scores a point. It's a contest between you and the stoop. The first one to reach a score of 100 points wins.

Two-Player Version

The two player version gives point values to each step: the bottom step counts for 5 points, the step above counts for 10 points, the step above that for 15 points, and so on for as many steps as there are. You throw the ball the same way, only this time it must bounce once before it's caught. A successful corner ball gives you a whopping 25-point bonus! But beware—if your opponent catches your ball, he can steal the points from you, and any ball is fair game for both. A foul or missed ball means no points for anyone. The first player to reach 100 points wins.

Seven Up

Players: 1
Materials: Ball
 Chalk
Surface: Paved
Special: High wall

There are seven steps to this handball game, each step a little more complicated than the one before. You play alone, with the wall your only real opponent. Draw a line about five feet from the base of a wall, and stand behind it. Then start with the first step, "onesies."

 For "onesies," throw the ball against the wall and catch it on the fly.

 For "twosies," throw the ball against the wall, but let it bounce once in front of the line before you catch it. Repeat.

 For "threesies," throw the ball against the wall and clap before you catch it on the fly. Repeat this two more times.

For "foursies," throw the ball against the wall, spin around, and catch it after the first bounce. Repeat this three more times, alternating the direction of your spin.

For "fivesies," throw the ball against the wall, clap twice behind your back, and catch it on the fly. Repeat this four more times.

For "sixies," throw the ball against the wall, get down in a push-up position, then jump up and catch the ball after the first bounce. Repeat only two times (Thank goodness!).

For "sevensies," throw the ball against the wall, clap your hands once in front and once in back, before catching the ball on the fly. Repeat this six times.

Each step and repetition that you complete counts as one point. If you go all the way from "onesies" to "sevensies" without a mistake, you've collected 25 points and win the game. But each miss gives the wall one point, too. Usually, by the time you've reached "sevensies," the score is something like: *You*: 18 points; *Wall*: 7 points. In this case, you continue the game—from "onesies"—until someone reaches a score of 25. Make sure the wall plays fair.

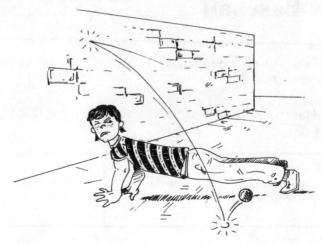

Four Square

Players: 4
Materials: Soccer ball or basketball
               Chalk
Surface: Paved

Draw an area about six feet square and divide it into four equal compartments. A player occupies each square. One player then bounces the ball into a neighboring square. The player in that square catches the ball and bounces it into another square, and so on. You could decide ahead of time to follow a particular sequence— for example, bouncing the ball only to the player on the right, or bouncing it to the right and then diagonally across—or you might decide to let each player choose a target. In any case, "Four Square" is lots of fun, especially when the pace heats up and the ball is flying!

If a player fails to catch a bounce in his square, the one who tossed it to him scores a point. The first player to reach a score of 21 wins.

Box Baseball

Players: 2
Materials: Chalk (optional)
Surface: Paved

"Box Baseball" is played across three sidewalk squares, like this:

California Angels	Strike Area	New York Yankees

Player #1 is the California Angels and Player #2 is the New York Yankees. Player #1 throws the ball into Player #2's box, passing it over the strike area. Player #2, standing outside his box, tries to catch the ball after one bounce. If he succeeds, it counts as an out for the Angels. But if he doesn't catch the ball after one bounce, each additional bounce means one more base for the Angels—so that two bounces mean a single; three bounces, a double; four bounces, a triple; and five bounces, a home run. If #1's throw bounces into the strike area, or misses #2's box, it's "Strike One," and he must throw again. Three strikes make an out, and it's #2's turn to throw.

After nine innings, the team with the higher score wins.

I Declare War

Players: 5–10
Materials: Ball
                 Chalk
Surface: Paved
Special: Large, clear area for running

This is a great game for quick thinkers and fast runners. Draw a big circle and divide it up into sections like a pie. Draw a smaller circle in the middle that can (if you're artistic) look like a globe. The slices represent different countries. Each player chooses a "country" and stands in that slice.

Select one player to be "It." If "It" is standing in a slice marked "Germany," then Germany declares war for this round. "It" starts the game holding the ball and saying: "I declare war on ———." Then "It" shouts the

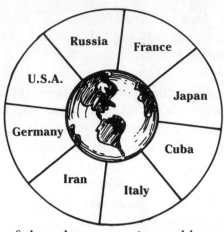

name of one of the other countries and bounces the ball as hard as possible in the middle circle. If Germany declares war on France, then everyone (including Germany) runs out of their countries and away from the circle—except France. France stays behind to catch the ball and yell "Freeze!"—stopping the others. France is then allowed to take three giant steps towards the closest player—Italy, perhaps—and throw the ball at him. If Italy is hit, he becomes "It" for the next round. But if France misses, all the players unfreeze and run back to their sections. At this point, France may throw the ball at the running players in a last ditch attempt to find another "It," but if she misses, she returns to her slice and declares war in the next round.

I Declare War—Elimination Style

In this version, France forces Italy out of the game if she scores a hit and then may take three more giant steps towards another player and throw the ball again. If she misses hitting the second player, everyone runs back to their countries. The last one home becomes "It" in the next round.

9

All Dressed Up & Something to Play

There you are, in your best clothes—just aching to play a good game. Maybe you're visiting, or waiting to go somewhere. Or maybe it's Sunday morning and you know how quiet everyone likes it. What do you do? The games in this chapter are exciting, but quiet—challenging, but not rough. All are designed for those occasions when you're dressed up—but determined to have fun anyway!

Hit the Coin

Players: 2
Materials: Ball
Coin
Chalk (optional)
Surface: Paved

This is a great Sunday morning ball game, perfect for those times when you don't want to run around too much and mess up your clothes. Place a coin on the crack between squares in the sidewalk. Or draw two boxes, each five feet square, and separate them with a straight line. One player stands in each box. The object is to bounce the ball on the coin, which scores one point. If your ball flips the coin over, you get two points and the chance to put the coin back on the dividing line, in case it has been knocked away from you. If you miss the coin completely, you continue to take turns bouncing the ball until someone scores a hit.

The first player to reach a score of 21 wins.

Categories

Players: 2–6
Materials: Ball
Chalk
Surface: Paved

You might think of this game as a continuation of "Hopscotch" (page 66) or "Potsy," using a ball instead of the "pot." Mark off a "court" with as many categories as you want—usually each player has a favorite.

Songs	Quarterbacks
Vegetables	Novels
Gems	Composers
Holidays	Rivers

Let's say you're first. You stand about four feet from the court and roll your ball into the square marked "Rivers." Then you run to catch the ball before it rolls into a neighboring square. If you don't stop it in time, your turn is over and the next player gets to roll the ball. If you do stop it in time, though, you step into the next square (Composers), bounce the ball once and call out a name in the category. For instance, as you step into the second square and bounce the ball, you might call out "Beethoven!" Then you step into the third square (Novels) and bounce the ball, saying maybe, "*The Great Gatsby!*" The step, the bounce, and calling the name, must all be done together. No player is allowed to linger in a square very long, and no name may be used twice.

If you stumble, or if your mind goes blank in some category (someone else's favorite, no doubt) you leave the court and must start from "Rivers" again, after all the other players have had a turn. If the next player gets through the court and back to "Rivers" without a mishap, he rolls his ball into "Composers" and starts walking around the court again, bouncing the ball and calling out a new name in each category.

If he walks through the court successfully, he rolls his ball into "Novels" and walks through again, and so on for the rest of the eight categories.

Whenever a player stumbles in a category, his turn is over. He must begin again by rolling his ball into the same category next time.

The first player to roll his ball and walk through all eight categories wins.

Nine Pins

Players: 2–5
Materials: 9 glass soda bottles, all roughly equal in size
                Croquet ball
Surface: Paved

"Nine Pins" is an old-fashioned bowling game. You need a slightly heavy, non-bouncing ball, like a wooden croquet ball. Place nine bottles like this:

The object of the game is to bowl over the bottles in the circle without knocking over the center bottle, which is called "Jack." Each bottle counts for two points, except for the Jack, which has no point value.

Take turns. You may walk around the circle, but you are never allowed to get closer to it than 12 feet. If you knock down one or more bottles on a single bowl, they are turned upright again, and you get another turn. But if you knock over the Jack, you must add up the point values of all the bottles you just knocked over and deduct them from your total score. Knocking down the Jack also ends your turn. A score of 21 wins.

Let's start a game with two players—Steve and Jill. Steve knocks down two bottles, but misses the Jack on his first turn. He gets four points and may bowl again. He knocks over a bottle *and* the Jack on his second turn, so he deducts two points from his total score of four, leaving him with two points and ending his turn. Now Jill tries. She knocks over a bottle and the Jack in her first turn and is given a *minus score*—minus two. It's Steve's turn again. This time Steve's bowl is a disaster— three bottles tumble over, taking the Jack with them. The three bottles added up to a score of minus six for that turn. Steve had a score of two, so he winds up with a score of minus four, giving Jill an odd sort of "lead." For the next turns Steve and Jill bowl cautiously, inching their way towards a winning 21.

If a player knocks over all eight bottles during a single turn without knocking over the Jack, he gets a 10 point bonus—and his turn is over.

Down the Lane

For a more challenging game, place the bottles no more than ten inches away from the Jack. Bowl "down the lane" at the bottles—that is, from behind a line about 15 feet away. The same bonus point rule applies for knocking over all the bottles during a single turn.

Shoebox Bowling

Players: 2–5
Materials: 7 marbles for each player
Shoebox
Scissors
Crayon
Stone
Surface: Paved (and smooth)

This is a great game to put together after you finish cleaning out your closet. Turn an old shoebox (without the cover) so that the open top faces the ground, and cut seven triangular holes into the side. Each hole should be just wide enough for a marble to pass through. Number the holes from one to seven, but in this order: place #1 over the center hole, #2 over the hole to the left of #1, #3 over the hole to the right of #1, #4 to the left of #2, #5 to the right of #3, and so on. In this way, you have the higher numbers placed closer to the edge of the box. Place a stone on top of the box to weigh it down.

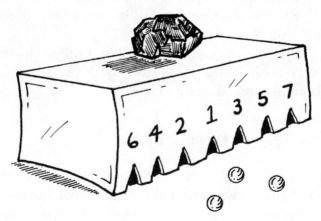

Now stand back about five feet and take turns bowling marbles into the shoebox. If your marble passes through one of the holes, you score the number of points written above the hole. If you miss the shoebox, or if your marble doesn't go into a hole, you are penalized two points and lose your next turn.

The first player to reach a score of 49 wins the game. If no player reaches a winning score after all have bowled their marbles, collect the marbles from inside the shoebox, pass them out and play again.

Animal, Vegetable, Mineral

Players: 4–10
Materials: Ball
Surface: Paved or grassy

One player—"It"—tosses the ball to another, calling out "Animal," "Vegetable," or "Mineral." The player who catches the ball must name something belonging to that group before "It" can count to five. For example, if "It" calls out "Animal!" and throws the ball to Joe, Joe must respond with a something like "Zebra!" or "Leather!" (made of animal skin) and return the ball before the count is up. If "It" calls out "Vegetable," tossing the ball to Sally, she must quickly respond with a word like "Broccoli!" or "Paper!" before returning the throw. And if Gus, next in line, catches the ball to "Mineral," he must come up with something like "Iron!" or "Water!" or "The Emerald City of Oz!" before he's off the hook. "It" may toss the ball to anyone and may even fake a throw now and then to keep people on their toes. If the players know each others' names, you may want to add names into the strategy. "It" could call out the name of one person, but toss the ball to someone else.

You may change the categories, if you'd like. Try playing with something like "Desserts," "Money" and "Movie Stars." A player might say "Hot Fudge" for the first category, "Francs" for the second, and "Clint Eastwood" for the third.

Any player who misses a catch is out of the game. A player who catches the ball but drops it—or goes blank and can't think of an object—becomes the new "It."

The last remaining player wins.

Coin Pitching

Players: 3–6
Materials: 5 coins for each player
Surface: Paved (facing wall)

Player #1 throws a coin against the curb or the lower part of a wall. Player #2 pitches one in the same way. If it lands within a handspan (from the tip of the thumb to the tip of the small finger) of Players #1's coin, Player #2 may claim it. If Player #2's coin is further away than a handspan, Player #3 follows, trying to throw his coin so that he may claim one or both of the coins that are out there. There's no limit to the number of coins you can collect if your coin falls a handspan away.

Continue the game until one player has all the "loot."

10
Spooky Games

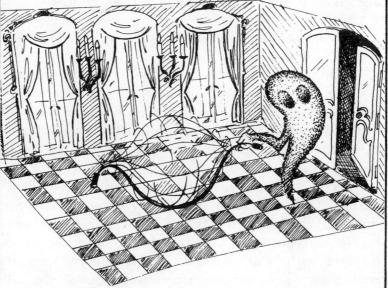

Do you like a good scare now and then? Are you the type who just can't resist a late night horror movie, though you know it'll spook your socks off? Do you go for the scariest rides at amusement parks? If so, then the games in this chapter are for you! Not only are they good tag and hiding games in their own right, but each game sets up an atmosphere of high anticipation and spookiness. They are best when played as daylight is fading and shadows are growing. For some, you even need a flashlight.

Boo Radish

Players: 5–10
Materials: Chalk or rope
Flashlight
Surface: Paved or grassy
Special: A large area, with lots of hiding places

Spooky noises and a flashlight add chills to this hide-and-seek idea.

Chalk out two boxes, each about five feet square. One box is a "churchyard" which serves as a home base, and the other is a "dungeon." Place the boxes about 20 feet apart. One player—"It"—holds the flashlight. He closes his eyes and counts to 50 while the others go off quietly to hide.

When the count is over, "It" ventures out with the flashlight, shining it towards every strange shape and shadow. When he suspects that a hiding player is close by, "It" calls out "Boo!", and all the hidden players must respond with "Radish!" The hidden players may disguise their voices or answer very softly, but all the calls "It" makes must be answered.

When "It" is closing in on a player, he shines his flashlight straight ahead, trying to catch the hider in the beam. If "It" succeeds, the player is captured and taken to the dungeon. If, however, a hiding player realizes that "It" is ready to close in, he may decide to rush out and make a dash for safety in the churchyard. If this player can tag a player who is being held in the dungeon, then both may run. Players who make it to safety in the churchyard may answer, "Radish!" too, hoping to confuse "It" and throw him off the trail.

If all players make it to the churchyard, then "It"

must repeat his role in the next game. If the last hider is frozen in the flashlight beam and captured, she becomes "It" in the new game. If, on the other hand, she rushes out and makes a dash for safety, "It" races her to the churchyard. The one who loses that race is the next "It."

Ghost Train

Players:	5–10
Materials:	None
Surface:	Paved or grassy
Special:	A large area, with obstacles to "duck" behind for quick hiding

In this game the players quietly disappear one by one, leaving an eerie, abandoned "Ghost Train" behind. Everyone forms a line, each holding the waist of the person in front. The first player—the "Engine"—starts moving forward at a fast trot, dragging its "passengers" behind. The line may snake around at various speeds and change directions, but all the passengers must look straight ahead and follow the Engine.

Then one by one, the last passenger in line quietly steals away to find a hiding space. Although all the players must look straight ahead and cannot glance back to see where anyone is hiding, the hiding player must be careful to choose a moment when the train is following a straight course. Otherwise, the train could twist around and bring the hiding player into full view of the others. If this happens, the Engine calls out the player's name and that player is out of the game. The engine, of course, is continually making sharp turns so it can see as much as possible.

After a while, only the Engine is left, chugging along. One by one, now, the hidden passengers try to get back on the train. The toughest job is that of the first passenger, who has to grab the waist of the Engine (giving him a good scare) before he realizes what is happening. If the Engine manages to yell, "Ghost Train," before the first passenger gets hold, the passenger becomes the Engine and the original Engine drops away to hide.

It works the same way every time a player is discovered trying to get back on the train. The train automatically reverses direction. The old Engine gets the chance to hide and the passenger who got caught becomes the new Engine.

Sometimes several passengers will manage to sneak back onto the Ghost Train making the line quite long again. But only the Engine may call "Ghost Train." Again, all players in line must look directly ahead and cannot glance around.

If all the hidden passengers manage to rejoin the train, the Engine must repeat that role in the next game.

Night Watchman

Players: 5–10
Materials: Chalk (optional)
Surface: Paved or grassy
Special: A slightly larger area needed here, with
              obstacles to duck behind, and places to hide.

In this hide-and-seek game, "It" stays in one place while the hiders quietly creep closer and closer, waiting for a chance to spring out at him. This game is also a good memory tester, and you'll see why! Play at dusk for the best results.

Choose one player to be the Night Watchman who stands at his post while the rest go off to hide. His post is a large circle drawn in the street or on the sidewalk, or it can be a tree trunk, or a porch step—any place will do, provided that it can be seen easily by everyone. The hiding players position themselves behind trees or lamp posts, and shift from one hiding place to another, as they sneak up on the Night Watchman.

Of course, the Watchman knows he is surrounded, and must keep every angle covered. When he spots a hider, he calls out that person's name. If he is correct, the players join him at his post and helps him to spot the others who are still lurking about. If he is wrong, the player whose name was mistakenly called becomes "immune" to his own name and must hereafter be called "Poindexter." This is a real predicament for the poor Night Watchman who must now remember who's who as well as who's where!

The Night Watchman wins if he (and his helpers, if any) can correctly call out the remaining players before they reach his post. He may then choose the next Night Watchman. He loses if someone manages to creep up and tag him, in which case the tagger shouts, "Free!" and all the remaining hiders rush to get inside the post. The last one inside becomes the next Night Watchman.

Wolves in the Woods _____

Players: 4–8
Materials: A large blanket
Flashlight (optional)
Surface: Grassy
Special: A large area—several back yards would be good—with plenty of hiding places

This spooky hide-and-seek game is best played when it's not too dark—about an hour after the sun goes down. If you play at night the game is a lot scarier, but you'll need a flashlight.

Divide the players into two teams: "Wolves" and "Campers." The Campers cover themselves completely with the blanket and count to a hundred, giving the Wolves a chance to hide. When the count is through, the Campers creep out in search of Wolves (with the flashlight, if you choose), leaving their safety blanket behind them in the shadows. Quietly, a wolf steals the blanket and hides it nearby while the other Wolves wait to *attack*! The only way the Campers can save themselves is to find the blanket and get back under it. Even when they find the blanket, though, it's usually so rumpled and knotted that quick shelter is impossible.

Wolves attack by tagging the Campers. Once a Camper is tagged, he becomes a Wolf, and goes off to hide with the other Wolves in the next round.

The game is repeated, each time with more Wolves and fewer Campers until all the Campers turn into Wolves. Change sides for the next game.

Aliens

Players:	**6–12**
Materials:	**None**
Surface:	**Paved or grassy**
Special:	**A large area—several back yards would be good—with plenty of hiding places**

If the thought of UFO's and creatures from outer space sends shivers up your spine, this is the game for you! It's particularly creepy to play at night, with just a few lamp posts or porch lights for illumination.

Mark out two Dens—a "Starting Den" and a "Safety Den." The Dens should be far apart and out of sight of each other. Assemble everyone inside the Starting Den and choose one player to be the "Alien." While the rest of the players cover their eyes and count to 100, the Alien goes off to hide somewhere between the two Dens. After the count is finished, one of the waiting players calls out: "Flying saucer! It landed in the woods!" This warns the Alien to keep low and still.

Now, one at a time, players leave the Starting Den and try to cross over to the Safety Den. Of course, to do this, they must pass through the area where the Saucer landed and the Alien is lurking. If the Alien jumps out of hiding and tags a crossing player, that player becomes an Alien too. Now both hide and wait for the next player to cross. If, on the other hand, the crossing player outruns the Alien and reaches the Safety Den, or if he never encounters the Alien *at all* during his cross, he waits in the Safety Den for the next player to join him. Players may choose to either run or walk across; but if the Dens are very far apart, each player should wait about a minute before following the player ahead of him. Another strategy is to sneak across—keeping out of sight of the Alien as you creep to the other side. But if you plan to cross this way, let the next player know so he'll give you a few extra minutes.

This is the eeriest part of the game. As each player disappears into the darkness ahead, you don't know whether *any* of them ever reach the Safety Den.

Players in the Safety Den have an important job to do now. As each player in the Starting Den begins to cross, he may choose to signal the safe players to find out how many (if any) have made it across to the Safety Den. If all the Safe players made it across, there's only one Alien out there and he may decide to walk across. If none of them have, and a small army of Aliens is waiting for him, he would have to change his strategy! The crossing player calls "Safe?" and the safe players must respond with a number. For example, if the crossing player is the fifth to venture out, there may be four safe players on the other side and only one Alien to watch out for. In that case, the players would respond with "Four!" If, on the other hand, all four players were tagged, and *five* Aliens were lurking, no one would answer the call. Of course, since the Dens are far apart, everyone must listen carefully.

At some point, there may be more Aliens than players waiting to cross. If so, the Aliens may creep up on the players in the Starting Den and then leap out at them for a final chase. Any player tagged before reaching the Safety Den becomes an Alien. Now every player is either safe or an Alien. Whichever side has the most players wins the game.

11
Crazy Games

The games in this chapter share a single purpose—to make the players laugh like hyenas! You'll find different sorts of games here—they don't require the highly organized or competitive kind of playing as the games in the previous chapters. Some, like "Laughing Loop," are hardly games at all—that is, they have no object and no winners and no losers. They're just funny, fun to do, and a good way to wind down the day's activities.

Selling Vegetables

Players: 5–10
Materials: None
Surface: Paved or grassy

This game was popular in San Francisco's Chinatown many years ago, and is probably very ancient. Choose two players, one is the "Buyer" and the other the "Seller." The remaining players are "Vegetables," who sit side by side, hands clasped tightly under their knees.

If you are the Buyer, you say to the Seller: "Hello, there! What's good today?" The Seller might answer: "Oh, the cabbages are fresh and the eggplants are great—come and see for yourself!" He takes you to the Vegetables, and you may squeeze and tickle each player saying, "Too soft!" or "Too hard!" You will try to "buy" the Vegetable that laughs, or the one that laughs the *hardest*. At this point, the Seller stands on one side, you stand on the other, and together you lift the Vegetable by the arms, swinging it back and forth three times. If the Vegetable can keep its hands clasped under its knees for three swings, you've lost it and the Vegetable goes back to its place. But if the Vegetable loses its grip, you get to buy it and take it out of the game. If you or the Seller loses hold of the Vegetable, whichever one dropped it is *replaced* by the Vegetable and the game begins again.

Magnetized

Players: 7–20
Materials: None
Surface: Grassy

This is one of those crazy games to play when everyone's too tired to run, and in the mood for a little silliness. Choose one player to be "It," who stands apart from the rest of the players. The remaining players drift about aimlessly, bumping into one another like zombies or sleepwalkers. Suddenly, "It" runs through the other players, tags one, and shouts "Magnetized!" All the other players cling to the magnetized player, usually knocking him down and piling on top of him. Then "It" shouts "Demagnetized!" and everyone gets up and begins drifting again.

"It" repeats this, each time running through the others and magnetizing a new player. When the players are tired of being magnetized, they can secretly agree (by whispering to each other while bumping) that the next time "It" runs through, everyone will pile on *him*—which puts a stop to that!

Laughing Loop

Players: 5–20
Materials: None
Surface: Grassy

The laughter in this game is contagious.

Player #1 lies on his back and places his head on the belly of Player #2. Player #2 then places *his* head on the belly of Player #3, and so on. Players wind up lying in a zig-zag formation, but the line should loop around so that the last player places his head on the belly of Player #1.

Now the fun begins. Player #1 shouts "Ha!" and Player #2 answers with "Ha, ha!" Player #3 shouts "Ha, ha, ha!" and Player #4 answers with "Ha, ha, ha, HA!" Of course, each time a player says "Ha," his belly bobs up and down, rocking the next player's head. It's a strange sensation! Soon, everyone loses control and starts laughing hysterically—and round and round it goes!

Pigs to Market

Players: 2–10
Materials: Broom handles or long sticks (one for each player)
Glass soda bottles (one for each player)
Chalk or rope
Surface: Paved or grassy

This racing game is tougher than it sounds, especially when you have more than three players—all of them zig-zagging in a mad dash for the finish line.

Players stand beside each other holding broom handles. In front of each player is a "pig," an empty glass soda bottle placed on its side. At the starting signal, the players must push their pigs along quickly with the broomsticks, trying to race in a straight line and keep out of each other's way—easier said than done!

The first player to reach the finish line wins the game.

Knots

Players:	10–20
Materials:	None
Surface:	Paved or grassy

"Knots" may look kind of funny, but it's actually a test of skill and coordination. That doesn't mean you won't have fun playing it, though. Players line up holding hands. The first player in line starts the knot by walking under the arms of two other players. The second player in line may choose to crawl through someone's legs. Of course, each player's moves affects every other player in the line—and soon there's an enormous tangle.

After the last player adds his bit of confusion, the trick is to untangle the knot without falling over or losing your grip. Any player who breaks hands with his neighbor is taken out of the knot—which makes things a *little* easier. But don't laugh too hard—or everyone tumbles and you're all out!

Leap Frog, Turtle Crawl

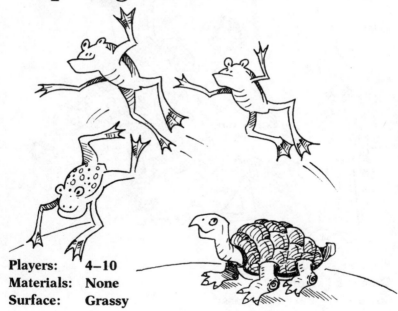

Players: 4–10
Materials: None
Surface: Grassy

Here's a new twist on an old favorite. Choose one player to be the "Caller." The remaining players stand in line about three yards from each other, waiting for directions. If the Caller yells "Leap Frog!", Players #1 and #2 (first and second in line) lean over, bracing their backs by gripping the upper part of their legs. Player #3 leaps over them, one at a time, straddling their backs and pushing himself over. Then he stops and leans over as the next player—the third in line—begins to leap.

This goes on for as long as it amuses the Caller. When he feels it's time for a change, he shouts, "Turtle Crawl!" and the next players must crawl through each other's legs, taking turns as before.

The Caller runs along beside the players, changing them from turtles to frogs and back again. Soon, someone says "Enough!" and the game is finished.

Rolling-Pin Race

Players: 7–11, but always an odd number
Materials: 2 ropes (each about 6 feet long)
Surface: Grassy

You've heard of rolling on the grass—and you've probably done it, too. But in this "rolling-pin" race, you do it with partners—and it's hilarious!

Mark out a starting line and a finish line with the ropes. Choose a referee who will give the starting signal and watch for a winner. The remaining players form two-player teams.

All the partners get into position behind the starting line, lying on the ground head-to-head. Both lie on their backs, and link hands overhead.

When the referee shouts "Go!" all the teams start rolling to the finish line. As they race, they usually turn in unexpected directions and run over each other before any one of them makes it to the finish line.

If partners get separated, they must take the time to put their rolling-pin back together before they can continue the race.

Knee-To-Chest Position

Sometimes, players prefer the knee-to-chest position for a sturdier, more controllable rolling-pin.

Here, Player #1 hooks his feet over #2's shoulders, and #2's feet are hooked over #1's shoulders. Each player hugs the legs of his partner tightly against his chest. You can roll a little faster this way. Of course, everyone must agree beforehand whether it's "link hands" or "Knee-to-Chest." Happy rolling!

Crab Race

Players: **3–10**
Materials: **2 ropes (each about 6 feet long)**
Surface: **Grassy**

Do you know how hard it is to walk like a crab? Well, running is even harder! Players line up behind the starting rope, which is stretched along the ground. But this is no ordinary race, because each player is a "crab." To get in the "crab" position, lie on your back and lift off the ground with your arms and legs tucked beneath you. It's peculiar—you have to look across your chest to see where you're going.

Choose a player to be the referee. He gives the "Go" signal and stands at the finish line as the crabs race by— a hysterical sight!

Limbo

Players: 6–10
Materials: Broom or broom handle
Surface: Paved or grassy

Choose two players who will hold opposite ends of the broom. Each end should rest on a player's upturned palm, so that the broom will fall to the ground if bumped from below. Start out with the broom about chest high.

One by one, the other players walk under the broom, making themselves shorter by stretching their legs apart and bending backwards. To get in the spirit, try doing it while the others clap in rhythm. A player who stumbles or knocks the broom down while going under it, is eliminated.

After all the players go under once, the broom-holders lower the broom to waist level, and the players take turns going under it again. With each repetition, the broom-holders drop the broom a little lower until they have to get on their knees. Eventually, all players but one are eliminated. That one wins the game.

12
Knock-You-Out Games

If you're not the type to tire out easily, these games are a fun way to use up that extra energy. Most involve a kind of organized tumbling around, and all—except for "Rooster Fight"—should be played on a grassy surface. A few are not games at all, really—"Pyramid Building," for example. But who could exclude human pyramids from a collection of classic backyard activities? Or the jolts and twists of "Snap the Whip," for that matter? Enjoy.

Whirligig

Players: 5–10
Materials: Long rope (at least 6 feet long)
Old shoe
Surface: Paved or grassy

A "whirligig" is a long piece of rope with an old shoe tied to one end for weight. One player holds the other end of the rope and spins around, so that the rope makes a sweeping circular motion. You'll see that even though the center player is standing, the weighted end of the rope swings close to the ground. The other players jump over the rope as it sweeps past them, and they are eliminated if they stumble. The center player may spin faster, bringing the rope higher. Everyone has to keep up!

Take turns spinning the rope.

Cowboys and Indians

Players: 10–20, but always an even number
Materials: Chalk or rope
"Treasure" for each team
Surface: Paved or grassy

Draw a line—or stretch a long rope—separating the Cowboy territory from the Indian territory. Cowboys and Indians stand about five feet from the boundary line, facing each other. In each team's territory is a "treasure" belonging to the opposite team, which is usually placed deep in "enemy" territory. The treasure can be an old shoe, or an empty soda can—anything that can be easily (and safely) carried away. If you're playing with lots of people, you can have several "treasures" scattered around.

The object of the game is for a Cowboy or an Indian to cross over into the enemy's space and reclaim the treasure—that is, bring it safely to his own side, without being tagged and captured.

Several players may cross over at the same time, but if a player is captured, he remains in enemy territory and must be rescued (tagged) by one of his teammates before any more of the treasure can be carried back across.

The first team to reclaim all of the treasure wins the game.

Treasure Maze

Players: 5–20, but always an even number
Materials: Chalk
"Treasure" for each team
Surface: Paved

This unusual game was invented thousands of years ago. Chalk out a large maze—about 40 feet square—according to this diagram:

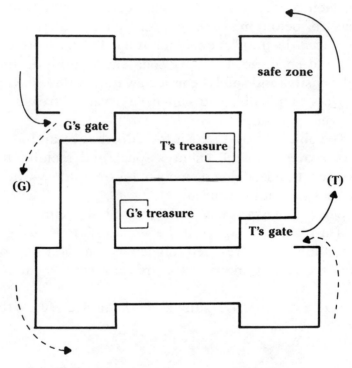

Divide the players into two teams. Then divide each *team* into "Guards" and "Thieves." The Thieves on each side want to steal a "Treasure" from the opposing team. They do this by leaving the maze one at a time, running around it, and then re-entering through the other team's gate. When Thieves leave the maze, they always run to their left so that they're going counter-clockwise and there are no collisions. This is important, since both teams may have Thieves running at the same time. Guards must wait inside the maze for invaders.

Let's take an example: if you're a Thief on the Turkish Team, you leave the maze through the gate marked "T," race around to the other side, and re-enter the maze through gate "G" (for Greeks, the enemy). Once inside, the Greek guards try to push you over a maze line, which would eliminate you from the game. But if you make it past them to the inner sanctum, you can grab their treasure—which turns out to be something like an empty peanut butter jar—and race back out. Once outside, you whip around the maze, enter through your own team's gate, deposit the treasure in your own inner room, and win the game for your team.

Remember—teams send out Thieves at the same time, so there's plenty of action on both sides of the maze. Guards may position themselves anywhere inside the maze, but must never leave it. Any Guard pushed over the maze line by a Thief is eliminated from the game.

Snap the Whip _____

Players: 7–20
Materials: None
Surface: Paved or grassy
Special: A slightly larger area, if you've got more than 10 players

This game is everyone's favorite. The longer the line of

players, the wilder the ride—especially for the player at the end!

Everyone lines up, holding hands. The first player in line runs as fast as he can, dragging the others behind him. He tries to "snap the whip" by making lots of sharp turns. Any player who breaks the line is eliminated.

Play until everyone is tired!

Pyramid Building

Players: 10–15
Materials: None
Surface: Grassy

Pyramid building is harder than it sounds. You need some strong backs and some good balancers. The reward is a magnificent human structure—short-lived though it may be!

The biggest players should make up the bottom row. If you're playing with ten people, the bottom row should be four players across—each on hands and knees and very close to his neighbor. The next row is made up of three players, also on hands and knees and packed close together. Each player in the second row straddles the crack between players in the bottom row, placing each knee on a separate player. The third row has two players, who straddle in the same way—and at the top of the pyramid is a single player.

Try taking your pyramid apart carefully, and then putting it back together with a different combination of players. But if you can't resist, and no one objects—let it crumble!

Skin the Snake

Players: 5–20
Materials: None
Surface: Grassy

You don't have to be a contortionist to "Skin the Snake." In fact, with a little practice, it's really a cinch. Players stand in line one behind the other and bend forward. Each player puts his right hand between his legs and grabs the left hand of the player in back of him. When everyone has a firm grip, the players walk slowly backwards. The player at the rear of the line lies on his back while one by one, the rest of the players straddle him and lie down behind him.

After you finish "skinning the snake," you might want to put it back together again. The last player to lie down gets up and walks astride the line, pulling up the next player—until everyone is back in line again.

Rooster Fight

Players: 6–20, but always an even number
Materials: Handkerchiefs or scarves, one for every other
                 player
Surface: Paved or grassy

"Rooster Fight" is a perfect name for this Mexican favorite. Every player tucks a handkerchief behind a belt or in a pocket—in a place where it can't be snatched away easily. Players pair off, facing their partners. Then each player holds his right arm up against his chest (grasping his left shoulder with his right hand), hops on the right foot, and tries to steal his partner's handkerchief. Partners must always face each other and may never run away. Pushing and bumping is allowed, but if a player drops his arm, or if his foot touches the ground, he is disqualified and out of the game.

When your handkerchief is stolen, you are out of the game. Winners wait for everyone to finish and then pair off for a final challenge.

Acknowledgments

Thank you to Eric Byron, Jill Earick, and Stephen Sturk for their recollections, and to Nancy Lowe and her son David for "trying things out." A special thanks to my editor and friend Sheila Anne Barry for putting it all together.

About the Author

When Glen Vecchione is not playing games or writing and illustrating books, he composes music for television and films. He made his theatrical debut as a composer on Broadway in 1981 with the jazz musical, *The Legend of Frankie and Johnny*. He is also a published poet and a desktop publisher: his magazine *Atafraxis* has introduced the work of many new authors.

A native New Yorker, Glen attended the University of California at Los Angeles and still spends part of the year on the west coast. Since he graduated Magna Cum Laude, he has worked as an actor, a playwright for children's theatre, a recording engineer and a music engraver. He has also travelled extensively throughout Europe and Asia, keeping a detailed record of his experiences.

Throughout his life, Glen has been keenly interested in urban folklore and plans to publish his material. He currently makes his home in New York City.

Age Range Chart & Index

AGE RANGE CHART & INDEX

Game	Page	Ages 6–8	8–12	13–18	Adult
Shadow Tag	8	★	★	★	★
Shadow Freeze Tag	9	★	★	★	★
Shoebox Bowling	94	★	★	★	★
Skin the Snake	123		★	★	★
Skully	69		★	★	★
Smugglers	26		★	★	★
Snake Eats His Tail	63	★	★	★	★
Snap the Whip	121	★	★	★	★
Squat Tag	14	★	★	★	★
Statue Tag	10	★	★	★	★
Stoop-Ball	83		★	★	★
Streets and Alleys	18		★	★	★
Touch Tag	11	★	★	★	★
Treasure Maze	120			★	★
Trivia Quiz Tag	12		★	★	★
Twos and Threes	56		★	★	★
Uncle Sam	33		★	★	★
What's the Time?	52		★	★	★
Whirligig	118		★	★	★
Wolf and the Sheep	55	★	★	★	
Wolves in the Woods	102		★	★	★